NO FREE LUNCH

SIX ECONOMIC LIES YOU'VE BEEN TAUGHT AND PROBABLY BELIEVE

CALEB S. FULLER, PH.D.

DEDICATION

To Frederic Bastiat

Seeking sophistry's end

The body of economic knowledge is an essential element in the structure of human civilization.

It rests with men whether they will make the proper use of the rich treasure with which this knowledge provides them or whether they will leave it unused. But if they fail to take the best advantage of it and disregard its teachings and warnings, they will not annul economics; they will stamp out society and the human race.

~ Ludwig von Mises

ACKNOWLEDGMENTS

Few write a book, no matter how small, without help and encouragement. As in the rest of our lives, we depend on the division of labor.

Peter Frank at Grove City College invited me to teach a short course on economic fallacies, which became the basis for this book. Thank you, Pete.

I'd also like to recognize Noah Gould, Rosolino Candela, and Jeff Herbener for their incisive editorial comments.

Lastly, thank you to all my teachers of economics, both in person and in print. You daily inspire.

TABLE *OF* CONTENTS

FOREWORD

Caleb Fuller's *No Free Lunch* is a welcome addition to a distinguished literature. This book takes its place among a pantheon of titles that strive to eradicate one of the greatest social ills humanity faces: *basic economic illiteracy*.

The book's title is captured in the story he tells in Chapter Two about Pareto and Schmoller at one of the first international meetings of economists. There, Pareto, the defender of economic theory, bests Schmoller in the story—as he should. The phrase "There are no free lunches" has been a staple of economists ever since.

Yet, communicating the basic principles of economics remains a challenge. As Henry Hazlit wrote many years ago, economic science faces two problems in communicating its basic teachings to the general public.

First, economics demands chains of reasoning that are often long and counter-intuitive, making it difficult for the untrained to work their way through to the correct conclusion. This requires a master teacher to aid the reader.

Second, precisely because there *are* those long chains of reasoning, the uninitiated are vulnerable to the manipulations of economics by powerful vested interests. That requires bold and brave individuals willing to upset the sensibilities of the mighty and the protected.

As Hazlitt did in his classic, *Economics in One Lesson*, Caleb Fuller carefully walks his reader through the basic logic of economics.

We live in a world of scarcity. The fact of scarcity implies that there are no solutions in economic life, only trade-offs. Prudent decision makers must learn to negotiate those trade-offs in a skillful manner. In pursuing that task, these decision makers rely on aids to the human mind that come in the form of property rights that incentivize, prices that guide, profits that lure, and losses that discipline.

Aided by private property, prices, and profit-and-loss, economic decision makers are constantly adjusting their behavior to changing circumstances, including changes in consumer tastes, technology, and resource availability. The ensuing market process works to coordinate the plans of a great multitude of buyers and sellers. Individuals are able to pursue productive specialization and realize peaceful social cooperation through exchange.

Disruptions to this process of exchange and production, on the other hand, result in bottlenecks—economists call them "shortages" and "surpluses"—that usually find their cause in the pathology of political privilege. Such privilege seeks to concentrate benefits on the well-organized and well-informed, while dispersing the costs on the unorganized and ill-informed. See Chapter Five for that logic.

This recognition of scarcity, and thus the necessity of trade-offs, is part of the "shock and awe" of economic reasoning. It is this truth about how the world works and its implications that opens eyes. But the lessons of economics reasoning that begin there do not necessarily end there.

Economics also teaches its readers about the beauty of complex coordination of the market system without central command. It also instructs about the hope that comes in the form of entrepreneurial discovery of new technologies, lower cost ways to meet existing consumer demands, and the creation of new products that satisfy the aspirations of others. The cornucopia of goods and services that comes with modern economic growth is driven by the entrepreneurial spirit and the social environment that unleashes that spirit.

This progress has lifted billions from the misery of extreme poverty over the last 25 years. As Matt Ridley is fond of pointing out, "Innovation is the child of freedom, but the parent of prosperity." The sort of economics that Fuller is teaching recognizes both aspects of that phrase.

And, finally, economics properly understood offers to the socially curious a way to direct their compassion in an effective direction. From Adam Smith to Caleb Fuller's presentation, economics is not a tool for the politically privileged to control and dominate their fellow citizens, but it is rather a critique of the powerful. It embraces "elbow room" for ordinary individuals to achieve extraordinary things. As they do so, they improve their lot in life as well as the lives of those in their families and communities.

No Free Lunch is a wonderful introduction to basic economic reasoning and its relevance to understanding how the world works. Read Fuller's lovely little book and be enlightened—it will open your eyes. It will instill a sense of awe at the beauty of market coordination, It will offer hope in the entrepreneurial recognition of opportunities for mutual betterment. And it will direct your compassion to the effective elimination of the social ills of poverty, ignorance, and squalor.

That is a lot to promise for an introductory book, but I don't do so lightly. The reason is that Caleb Fuller has offered his readers a wonderfully written invitation to inquiry into the worldly philosophy and science of economics. If you accept his invitation, those promises will be fulfilled.

Peter J. Boettke
University Professor of Economics and Philosophy
BB&T Professor for the Study of Capitalism
George Mason University

INTRODUCTION

Every man knows there are evils in the world which need setting right. Every man has pretty definite ideas as to what these evils are. I, too, have a pet little evil, to which in more passionate moments, I am apt to attribute all the others. This evil is the neglect of thinking. And when I say thinking, I mean real thinking, independent thinking, hard thinking.

~ Henry Hazlitt

I accidentally wrote this book.

Last winter, I filmed a video series on "everyday economic errors" for Grove City College. When I asked my friend Rosolino Candela to review my video script, he suggested that I'd written a book.

You're holding the results of Rosolino's offhand remark.

The book is an accident, but its topic is not. Economics changed my life. That's not a sentence you've likely heard before. But I wish more people could say it. Ultimately,

NO FREE LUNCH ● CALEB S. FULLER

that's why I agreed to create the videos on economic errors, and it's why I converted them to book format.

Most people don't think economics can be life-changing because they confuse economics with forecasting, charts, diagrams, numbers, ideology, math, business, statistics, money, finance, stock markets, personal finance, or even "the economy."

Yuk.

If I thought economics was synonymous with any of those, I'd never have become an economist. I wouldn't waste time reading economics books.

But economics is about people—how they pursue their goals, whatever those goals are. It's also about what hinders them in their goal pursuit. Good economics takes people as they really are; sometimes selfish, sometimes altruistic; at times knowledgeable, mostly ignorant; occasionally foresighted, typically myopic; cold and calculating in instances, but more commonly impulsive and emotional.

If people, real-world people, plus their goals, hopes, dreams, and aspirations don't interest you, check your pulse.

In my experience, no one is disinterested by the social world that humans inhabit. But many are too easily persuaded by superficial analysis, by bumper-sticker slogans that fail to grapple with the rich complexity of human society. A little more curiosity, a little more awe, would go a long way in dispelling these surface-level catchphrases. As it is, we too often settle for watchwords that only cloud our vision, exacerbating the shortsightedness to which we're already prone.

If anything, we need a pair of eyeglasses that can extend our vision beyond where we're accustomed to looking. I'm hopeful my little book can provide you with just those glasses. To calibrate them, I've selected six common, consequential, and unfortunately pithy misconceptions about how the social world operates. I picked the *No Free Lunch* cover because these mistakes all center on neglect of that most foundational economic concept: opportunity cost.

I'll be forthright: I consider these errors to be worse than mere misconceptions or missteps. I think they're lies. Allow me to explain.

To begin, these fallacies have been around for a while, giving many generations the opportunity to ponder and scrutinize them. When I say "a while," I don't mean "since 1995." They're as old as time.

Aristotle and Aquinas held some of these mistakes, as did many of your other favorite intellectuals whom I won't name. They had an excuse; we don't. They lived and died before the discipline of economics had gotten a chance to shed light on the social order.

Since we're several centuries removed from economics' founding (no matter when you reckon the date), we'd best wise up. If we repeat these errors in 2021, we'll be spreading lies. You won't have to look hard for the lies—they're my chapter titles.

Knowledgeable readers will detect the tremendous debt I owe to economics' greatest communicators, specifically Frederic Bastiat (1801–1850) and Henry Hazlitt (1894–1993). At the risk of causing you to put my book down to pick up theirs (a risk I'm willing to take—I might even recommend it), little I say here is original.

Yet, since their lessons have clearly not been heeded, I figured they could be uttered one more time with feeling: "It takes varied iterations to force alien concepts upon reluctant minds."[1]

In this little book, I avoid that most ugly of dialects, "economic-ese." Everything is written in plain English, the way I think economics should be.

The dismal science has fallen on hard times recently, suffering assaults both from within and without. These attacks usually begin by asserting economics is no science at all. I disagree but make no attempts at a methodological defense. My only goal is to persuade by showing the power and beauty of economic reasoning.

Nor do I attempt to answer the many objections that not-so-wise guys love raising to the reasoning presented in this book. It's my belief that all—yes all—of these objections have failed to internalize the basic lesson before going on to develop a counterargument. As a result, the comebacks fail. I believe economic reasoning is airtight. When you think you've heard a zinger, go back to the basics—and cogitate for a bit.

Caleb S. Fuller
Assistant Professor of Economics
Grove City College
Grove City, PA

CHAPTER ONE

DESTRUCTION IS PROFIT

I'm sad when stuff breaks.

~ My niece, Jess, age 6

An Economic Eye Exam

No one likes eye exams.[2] I've even experienced fitful nights of sleep, all due to that dreaded puff of air scheduled to befall me the following day.

Despite our discomfort, we keep going back to the eye doctor. Any economist will heartily affirm that actions speak louder than words. Our repeated visits to the optometrist say that we value our sight supremely. If we have it, we'll do almost anything to keep it. For those who regain sight, their joy is palpable.

I feel that way about economics. The much-maligned, much-avoided economics is actually like a pair of powerful lenses. Without the framework economics provides, most of us are groping about in the dark when we think about the social world. Tragically, our short-sighted view of social life causes us to make many errors in our reasoning.

As you'll see in this book, economic errors—lies—about the social world usually aren't innocuous. Often, they're a matter of life and death. Economics is fun. But it's fun of the deadly serious type.

In just a few sentences, your first economic eye exam will begin. By the end of this book, you'll have acquired a script that will rectify possibly patchy parts in your vision of the social world.

Open your eyes wide. Focus on that colorful hot air balloon. You'll feel a puff of air. It shouldn't hurt.

But it might be uncomfortable.

Myopia

On September 14, 2001—not three full days after the 9/11 attacks—Paul Krugman wrote the following words in the pages of the *New York Times*:

It seems almost in bad taste to talk about dollars and cents after an act of mass murder. Ghastly as it may seem to say this, the terror attack—like the original day of infamy, which brought an end to the Great Depression—could even do some economic good. Now, all of a sudden, we need some new office buildings. Rebuilding will generate at least some increase in business spending.[3]

Is Krugman right that there was an economic silver lining to the 9/11 attacks? While we're at it, did the "original day of infamy" bring an end to the Great Depression? If you want to know the answers to those questions, keep reading.

While most Americans remember little from high school, most seem to recall that we'd still be languishing in the doldrums of the Great Depression without World War II. When you first heard that claim, something about it should have rubbed you the wrong way. By the end of this chapter, you ought to know exactly why it bothered you.

As it turns out, you were subjected to educational malpractice. But I don't want to be too hard on your teacher. Economics is a breeding ground for life's subtlest errors in reasoning. Repeated often enough and believed widely enough, they attain the status of "folk wisdom." They're anything but.

I'm not the first to note the way economic lies proliferate. "Economics," observed Henry Hazlitt in the foreword to his 1946 book, *Economics in One Lesson*, "is haunted by more fallacies than any other study known to man."[4] Hazlitt attributes these widespread lies to "the persistent tendency of man to see only the immediate effects of a given policy ... and to neglect the long-run effects of that policy. It is the fallacy of overlooking secondary consequences."

Hazlitt's observation is profound, but it's not particularly original. He's channeling the memorable Frederic Bastiat, a nineteenth-century economist and iconoclast. Bastiat's initial take is even better than Hazlitt's. It's broader and more comprehensive. A myopic focus on the immediate and visible effect isn't just limited to analyzing public policies. It threatens to blind us whenever we analyze the social world.

In Bastiat's 1850 words:

In the sphere of economics an action, a habit, an institution or a law engenders not just one effect but a series of effects. Of these effects, only the first is immediate; it is revealed simultaneously with its cause, it is seen. The others merely occur successively; they are not seen; we are lucky if we foresee them. The entire difference between a bad and a good economist is apparent here. A bad one relies on the visible effect while the good one takes account both of the effect one can see and of those one must foresee.[5]

If Dr. Bastiat had to diagnose what afflicts our economic vision, he'd say "myopia."

This book examines six of the most common economic lies, all of which result from a blinkered focus on the "visible effect" while ignoring the effects that "must be foreseen."

At some point, someone taught you to believe each of these lies, and what's worse is that you probably believe them. To help you see through these economic lies—such as the idea that the 9/11 attacks provided a boost to our economy—this book will provide you with a pair of powerful "economic eyeglasses."

I'm passionate about helping you reject these six lies because this is much more than an intellectual exercise for me. Here's why: Each of these lies undergirds public policies that harm real human beings.

As you begin to read, I only ask one thing: that you attempt to put on this pair of eyeglasses. Make them yours. These eyeglasses will focus your attention on the core economic concept of opportunity cost. That's it. We'll use a single tool to help us see through economic lies that refuse to die. I call this perspective the "opportunity cost lens." I'll define what I mean by that in just a few pages.

Of course, if you find that these eyeglasses make the world blurrier instead of clearer, nothing can stop you from discarding them.

I don't suspect that'll be the case. After all, everyone views the world through some kind of lens. So the only question is: Does your lens help you see the world more clearly? Or does it exacerbate the shortsightedness that Bastiat identifies?

Here's an example. Most folks believe that we can obviously improve safety by licensing electricians. That way, unqualified people aren't messing around with dangerous wires.

Not so fast—as we'll see in the third chapter of this book, the opportunity-cost lens reveals that this is a lie. If you too assume that licensing must improve safety, perhaps the lens you're looking through isn't calibrated. Or maybe it's smudged and needs to be cleaned. Either way, I want to help you get a fresh pair of glasses that enables you to see the world more clearly.

The opportunity cost lens offers a systematic way of thinking that promises to supplant "folk economics"—a term coined by Emory University economist Paul Rubin.[6] "Folk economics" consists of the blurry lenses we peer through as we make sense of complex reality. Often, these lenses overlap in ways that are contradictory or inconsistent. Thankfully, the opportunity cost lens shows us the way out.

James Buchanan, the 1986 winner of the Nobel Prize in Economics, puts it this way: "What [economics] does ... is simply allow the average man, through professional specialization, to command the heights of genius." Buchanan says that without the economic lens, we risk becoming: "a jabbering idiot, who makes only noise under the illusion of speech."[7] Yikes! That's a fate this book will help you avoid.

You might be wondering why you should risk trading your old, dusty lenses in for the opportunity cost lens. Aren't economists themselves a bunch of "jabbering idiots" who can't agree on anything? That's certainly the public perception of economists. But it's simply not true.

The empirical evidence suggests a gulf between what professional economists believe about the world and the average person's beliefs. Economists simply see the world through a different lens.

Bryan Caplan, an economist who has studied public opinion extensively, documents these differences in a 2002 paper. He finds that the American populace's economic beliefs differ in statistically significant ways from what economists believe. Importantly, economists exhibit a marked consensus on fundamental economic questions, even when Caplan controls for their ideological commitments or political party affiliations, such as whether they're a registered Republican or Democrat.

Economics is an equal opportunity offender. Conservative or liberal, rich or poor, religious or skeptical, you'll find economics mounting serious challenges to many widely held and cherished beliefs.

Consider just one example from Caplan's research: The average American is far more likely than economists to blame gasoline price increases on seller greed. Economists prefer a supply-and-demand explanation. As Caplan puts it, "Anyone with a Ph.D. in economics, rich or poor, left or right ...would resist the 'greed explanation' for prices." In other words, there is a distinct and identifiable "economic point of view."

As Deirdre McCloskey writes in the introduction of *The Applied Theory of Price*, "You wouldn't know it from the image of economists as a confused mob of social forecasters ... but economists agree about a surprisingly large number of things."[8]

I don't intend to suggest unanimity among economists any more than it exists among biologists or theologians. Still, consensus on fundamental issues reflects a core economic way of seeing the world.

I also don't wish to suggest that professional economists can't make errors. They make plenty of them. The economist Paul Krugman is making one in his *New York Times* column. Instead, I simply suggest that when economists do fall into traps like Krugman's, they're often straying from the consensus principles they profess in their textbooks. It appears that Krugman must have left his economic eyeglasses on his bedside table the day he wrote that column.

I disagree with other economists all the time. When I do, it's usually because I think they have a severe case of myopia that only a hard-nosed economic analysis can cure.

Lessons from a Smart-Aleck

If myopia is the diagnosis, what's the solution? Every myopic patient will experience an improvement in vision immediately with the "opportunity cost lens." So what is it? What does it do for us? A story is the best way I know to give you a first peek through these powerful glasses.

It's not my story. Frederic Bastiat gave us the "parable of the broken window" in an essay memorably titled "That Which Is Seen, and That Which Is Not Seen."[9] In the story, we meet a beloved shopkeeper who finds that a teenage vandal has thrown a brick through his window. A crowd gathers. Along with the shopkeeper, they lament this senseless act of destruction.

Eventually, a voice from the crowd—a bit of a smart-aleck—pipes up and offers a different take on the day's events. He says:

Wait a second, guys. There's a silver lining here. The shopkeeper must hire our local glazier to repair the window—and this will increase our windowmaker's income. Our glazier will take his new income and buy a suit from our local suit-maker. The suit-maker will then spend his new income on our local cobbler for a pair of shoes. This process won't stop until everyone in our village sees their incomes rise. This vilified teenager is nothing short of a philanthropist.

As with your high school teacher's claims about World War II, the smart-aleck's reasoning shouldn't sit well with you. If he was right, what would the implications be?

For starters, we're not beholden to teenage vandals' schedules to generate prosperity. As I tell my students at Grove City College, we could do our good deed for the day by ending class early, marching downtown, and throwing bricks through all the shopkeepers' windows. More prosperity for our community. At some schools, I'd have to be careful about what I suggest; but thankfully, my students aren't prone to acts of destruction.

Plus, they see this for the lousy argument that it is.

To push the smart-aleck's conclusion a bit further, we might ask him: "Why is Sub-Saharan Africa still so poor?" If bringing prosperity were as easy as he suggests, every region of the world would be only a few smashed windows away from widespread prosperity. And if bricks are good, wouldn't tanks or a full-blown aerial assault be better?

What's conspicuously missing from the wise guy's analysis is our book's bedrock concept: opportunity cost. Opportunity cost is the value of the alternative you sacrifice when you choose to pursue a goal—any goal.

Put another way, "opportunity cost" is the flip side of every choice you make. By choosing to read this book, you're sacrificing some other goal you could pursue right now, such as reading some other, more entertaining book. When you use a stick of butter for baking a cake, you're sacrificing the chance to bake cookies with that butter.

Somehow I doubt he cared much for economics, but I like Henry David Thoreau's poetic understanding of opportunity cost that he expresses in his classic book, *Walden.*[10] Thoreau says, "The cost of a thing is the amount of what I will call life which is required to be exchanged for it." In other words, cost is deeply personal. Your cost is whatever you value and whatever you sacrifice whenever you make a choice.

What makes opportunity cost tricky is that it's "invisible." It requires "economic eyeglasses" to even notice that it exists. Our sacrificed goals never materialize. They live in our minds, but they exist nonetheless.

Now, there's a reason why opportunity cost is such a fundamental concept in economics. A seemingly mundane insight, opportunity cost reasoning contains tremendous explanatory power. For example, why are lines—such as the checkout line at the grocery store—longer in poorer neighborhoods? Opportunity cost. Poorer individuals sacrifice less in foregone wages when standing in line and prefer longer lines to higher prices. Stores are merely responding to consumer demand.

Speaking of food, why do retirees spend fewer dollars on their meals but also spend more time cooking them? At this point, you've probably guessed the answer: Opportunity cost, again. Retirees sacrifice less in foregone income when they spend time in the kitchen than do those in their working years.

Finally, why have women historically attended religious services in greater numbers than men? Are they simply more pious? Maybe they are. Or maybe men's opportunities in labor markets have historically been better and have thus increased the opportunity cost of participation in religious life.

Fair enough, so opportunity cost explains many of the little puzzles of life. But, how does it shed light on the big questions? Can it explain why vandalism and 9/11 didn't make us better off?

Yes. Simply put, the concept of opportunity cost tells us that all resources have alternative uses. To understand this point, let's revisit the smart-aleck's argument. Bastiat counters the not-so-wise guy by asking us to imagine what our shopkeeper would have done with his money had the window not been smashed. Perhaps he would have visited the suit-maker who, in turn, would have bought new shoes from the cobbler. But this economic activity never materializes because the shopkeeper is spending on window repair instead.

At this point, a clever person might object, "This just sounds like a wash. In Bastiat's reply to the smart-aleck, the shopkeeper gives money to the glazier instead of the suit-maker. What's the difference from the perspective of the community as a whole?"

This objection fails to look through the opportunity cost lens and therefore fails to identify the actual cost of the vandal's destruction.

The key point is that the vandal's misbehavior means that this community must now devote labor and resources just to restore the status quo—before there were any broken windows. Don't forget, though, that the glazier's labor is a valuable resource with alternative uses. Likewise, the materials he uses to create the window and the windowpane could contribute to other building projects. Had the window remained intact, our glazier would have been hard at work creating a window for a new shop across the street.

Instead, the glazier is working, yes, but merely to restore the standard of living that the community enjoyed before. As a result, the glazier is not creating new goods that allow people to satisfy their unfulfilled desires.

The vandal did not make the community better off. The actual cost of his destruction is all the things we can't see but would have gotten had he behaved himself. When community members devote resources and labor to repairing the window, the cost is that they can't devote those same resources to creating something else.

As Bastiat summarizes the lesson, "Destruction is not profit." Bastiat's parable teaches us to lament the vandal's act, and not because "the economy" got "worse" in some vague, undefined way. The economy is nothing more and nothing less than you and I trying to achieve our goals. The vandal in the story has taken the people in his community one step further from achieving their plans.

There are fewer hospitals, fewer books, less chocolate, fewer pure-bred puppy dogs, and less of anything else humans desire in the vandal's world. At the risk of sounding melodramatic: When windows break, people die.

Debunked over 170 years ago, the "Broken Window Fallacy" has yet to have its well-earned funeral. I began this book with a contemporary example of the Broken Window Fallacy on a massive scale. Let's use our opportunity cost lens to assess Krugman's claim that the destruction of 9/11 had an economic upside. Yes, 9/11 generated a flurry of concentrated and highly visible economic activity in one particular sector—construction. Contractors hired workers in droves to clear the sites of rubble and begin the rebuilding process.

Wearing our economic eyeglasses, we might ask, "Where did all the construction workers come from? What about all the tools and materials?" The answer is that they came from other areas of the economy. What would these workers have been doing if 9/11 had never happened? They'd have been building new homes, new office buildings, and new restaurants.

Sadly, these creations only exist in our minds precisely because those workers devoted their efforts to the 9/11 clean-up. We could ask a similar question about all the equipment used during clean-up and rebuilding, everything from sophisticated machinery to pedestrian hammers and nails.

What new, valuable goods and services would have been created with all that labor, materials, and equipment? We'll never know.

The Broken Window Writ Large

Like man-made disasters, natural disasters also offer ample opportunity for those with dirty eyeglasses to see an economic upside where there is none. For example, a 2011 *Politico* piece stated, "Hurricane Irene might have provided some short-term economic stimulus as billions of dollars will likely be spent to repair the damage to the East Coast over the weekend."[11]

I could go on, quoting story after story that reports on the supposed economic benefits created by natural disasters, but you can also find countless examples for yourself. As an exercise, pay attention the next time you see a story describing a hurricane. Without fail, some intrepid journalist will find a "silver lining" stemming from a supposed "economic boost." The "boost" isn't real. It's an illusion created by dirty eyeglasses.

Unsurprisingly, empirical research confirms that disasters aren't a boon. In 2014, economists Solomon Hsiang and Amir Jina published a paper titled "The Causal Effect of Environmental Catastrophe on Long-Run Economic Growth: Evidence from 6,700 Cyclones."[12]

Their paper examines thousands of cyclones around the world between 1950 and 2008. The authors find that "the data reject hypotheses that disasters stimulate growth.... Instead, we find robust evidence that national incomes decline, relative to their pre-disaster trend, and do not recover within twenty years."

Bastiat would have told you something similar in 1850.

Day of Infamy

If you've been tracking, you now know sufficient economics to see through the biggest Broken Window Fallacy of them all—the idea that the original day of infamy brought an end to the Great Depression.

Yes, World War II generated many highly visible, easy-to-identify-without-any-special-eyeglasses economic activities—just as hurricanes do. Ten million men were drafted into the military, with women primarily taking their place in the workforce. Factories began churning out tanks, guns, and ammunition—often at the explicit command of the government. However, it's important to grasp that increases in physical output are not synonymous with increases in wealth.

To see why, think about what comprised the war-time output. Tanks, guns, and ammunition aren't goods that cause the consumer's standard of living to rise. You can't eat tanks, guns, and ammo. Nor can you wear them. They don't directly increase the amount of leisure time at your disposal. Imagine for a moment that every worker and every machine in the economy began producing guns. Perhaps the sheer quantity of physical output would rise.

What would happen to our living standards? They'd fall. No more clothes, food, or cars.

The situation wasn't that extreme. Americans did, though, enjoy less clothing, less food, and fewer cars. As a result of the war activity, the average U.S. citizen's standard of living fell during the war years—a particularly notable statistic since the preceding decade was the worst depression in global history.

Economic historian Robert Higgs shows in a 1992 paper that real consumption per U.S. citizen declined by six percent between 1941 and 1943.[13] As Higgs thoroughly documents, consumers' lives got worse in other harder-to-detect ways, too.

For instance, with fewer civilian cars being produced and gas and rubber being rationed, the mundane task of commuting to work became a hurdle for many. Among other things, this prompted many Americans to make the costly move to urban centers. Why did living standards fall so much during the war years? Look through the opportunity cost lens again.

If the war hadn't been ongoing, what would most of the military men have been doing? They could have been producing. And what about all the materials devoted to wartime production of uniforms, tanks, and weapons instead of new shoes, cars, and household appliances? Therefore, we shouldn't be surprised when we see the decrease in living standards borne out empirically.

Robert Higgs, who I mentioned a moment ago, "disaggregates" the Gross Domestic Product (GDP) statistic to see which portion of our economy's output is government spending—driven mainly by the war effort— and which is attributable to private activity. What Higgs finds destroys the conventional narrative. In 1942, America entered the war. Indeed, GDP rose significantly in the following months. This increase is responsible for the myth that World War II ended the Great Depression.[14]

But it's crucial to look at what's happening to private GDP. It drops as the government begins swallowing more and more private economic activity. GDP remains elevated during the war years, but the private economy's share continues to plunge. That's not just data. It tells a human interest story. The living standards of real human beings, as measured by "private GDP," fell unambiguously due to the war effort.

Some would say that the war effort justified any amount of suffering and that the opportunity cost was worth it. That may very well be true. Whether or not the outcome was worth the cost is beside the point. We must recognize the wartime standard of living for what it was: suffering. It might have been necessary to defeat Hitler, but the war did not raise living standards in the United States.

Recovery from the Great Depression only began in 1945, when the war ended. It reached a crescendo in 1946 as private activity—and living standards—rebounded. That pattern is what we'd expect if we look through the opportunity cost lens. After all, the war's conclusion saw the government releasing key resources—both men and materials—back to the private sector, where they got back to work raising our living standards.

Congratulations. You just learned your first lesson in opportunity cost: Destruction isn't profit. Now, when you hear journalists or pundits or even economists talking about the silver lining of destruction, you'll be able to see right through their claims. Just think: "What would these resources have been doing if this disaster hadn't happened?"

In the next chapter, we'll continue calibrating our economic eyeglasses by correcting another lie that arises when we ignore opportunity cost. We'll examine the falsehood that "lunch is free."

CHAPTER TWO

LUNCH IS FREE

When you get something for nothing, you just haven't been billed for it yet.

~ Franklin P. Jones

Aha!

Two nineteenth-century thinkers were arguing. While Italian Vilfredo Pareto was presenting his work at an academic conference, German Gustav Schmoller repeatedly interrupted him to claim that there were no such things as universal economic laws.

Although the argument took place in the late nineteenth century, it's evergreen. In fact, as the contemporary economist Israel Kirzner once put it, "The great debate in the history of economics has been between those who understand the nature of economic law and the deniers of economic law."[15] You could say that Schmoller was a world-famous economic law denier.

Annoyed by Schmoller's antics, Pareto was determined to prove him wrong. Later in the day, Pareto disguised himself as a beggar and waited for Schmoller to pass him on the street. Once Schmoller was in earshot, Pareto accosted him: "Sir, I'm a poor beggar. Do you know anywhere in this city where I could get a free lunch?"

Schmoller replied, "Dear sir, I know of many places where you may have a lunch for very cheap—but there is no place where a lunch may be had for free."

It was at this moment that Pareto is said to have leaped up and shouted: "Aha! So you do believe in economic laws!"[16]

This story suggests two important ideas. First, academics used to have a much better sense of humor than they do now. Second, this story illustrates another foundational economic concept. In fact, it's the concept that's responsible for opportunity cost. That concept is scarcity. It's a simple word, but it can also be the source of tremendous confusion when it's not defined correctly. Something is "scarce" if you can't get it without bearing an opportunity cost.

Here's another way to put it: A thing is "scarce" when it's in limited supply and also desirable. An autographed baseball is scarce, as are bananas. You must give something up, even if it's just time in the case of harvesting wild bananas, to get them. Acquiring bananas incurs an opportunity cost. By contrast, a virus that's in limited supply—but which nobody wants—might be "rare." It's not "scarce."

"Scarcity" can be a slippery concept, so I want to take yet another crack at it. If we didn't have to bear an opportunity cost to get something, it'd be genuinely free to acquire in nature and thus not scarce. Clean air in most places isn't scarce. It is scarce while scuba diving and while visiting the moon, Los Angeles, or Beijing.

Scarcity is why "there's no such thing as a free lunch." When something's scarce, there will always be some way of allocating it among all the competing uses for it. For example, beachfront real estate is both in limited supply and highly desirable. There are competing uses and users for it. It's scarce. Therefore, there will be some system for deciding who gets to use the real estate and for what purpose. That's not optional.

Scarcity implies the ubiquity of competition. You can't abolish competition for resources without eliminating scarcity itself. Since we're stuck with some form of competition, the question becomes: What system will people use to compete for scarce resources?

Humankind's Greatest Invention

Prosperous societies use market prices to allocate scarce items. People compete for those resources through their willingness to outbid others by offering a higher price.

In a nutshell, when something becomes more desirable relative to the existing supply, its price rises. The higher price allocates the good to those who value it most highly. For instance, most of us don't own yachts only because the price is prohibitive. The yachts get allocated to Bill Gates and not to me because he's able and willing to pay the price. I'm not.

Compared to the price system, every other system people have thought of for allocating scarce resources seems to have severe shortcomings. We could compete for scarce items violently. "Might makes right"—whoever's stronger gets the good. We might ask who would produce anything in such a world. An even more sophisticated question would be: How would we know what to produce? See Chapter Six for more on that question.

We might allocate based on need, as Karl Marx suggested. Yet, isn't "need" arbitrary, and who will determine your needs? Perhaps we could allocate based on "merit"—but even my very intelligent philosopher friends can't agree on who's meritorious. I'm certainly not going to pretend to know.

We must choose one of these systems for allocating goods. Using prices to allocate goods isn't perfect, in the sense that scarcity is always with us in this "vale of tears." But using prices sure beats the alternatives. Under the price system, people compete for goods peacefully and productively. And under the price system, goods eventually wind up in the hands of those who value them most highly.

Winston Churchill once described democracy as "the worst form of government—except for all the others."[17] I like to tell my students, "The price system is the worst system for allocating scarce resources—except for all the others."

It's my opinion that the price system is humankind's greatest invention. While I've heard arguments for such contenders as the wheel, the lightbulb, or even the legal system, I remain skeptical that these rival the wonders of the price system.

Economists' praise for prices notwithstanding, many people believe that we could make goods more available simply by forcing the price lower. Perhaps we should dispense with the price system altogether. In other words, maybe the price is the only thing preventing us from having a free lunch. If only the price were zero—or at least closer to it— more people could enjoy more goods.

Free-lunch thinking manifests itself most clearly in public support for price ceilings. Price ceilings exist whenever the government dictates a maximum price that sellers can charge.

As economist Thomas Sowell puts it, "Economists have long been saying that there is no free lunch. Controlling prices creates the illusion of free lunches."[18]

But the illusion is just that. It's fake. All scarce goods have to be allocated somehow. If they aren't allocated according to a person's willingness to pay the price, they'll be allocated on some other basis.

I said this a moment ago, but it's worth repeating: Under the price system, buyers compete with one another by offering higher prices. When they can't do that, they'll simply compete in some other way. They'll incur opportunity costs as they do. Lunch isn't free—even if you make the price zero.

When we ignore opportunity cost, we end up grounding policies in false utopias instead of in reality. One such policy is rent control, where the government sets a maximum price for housing units. This policy has seen a surge in popularity in recent years, with places including California, Oregon, Washington D.C., and New York introducing expanded rent control legislation. For the rest of this chapter, we'll explore how rent control policies fail to deliver a free lunch, even as they mandate a lower money price for housing.

Is the Rent Too Damn High?[19]

Rent control seems like a commonsense policy if your goal is to help the poor tenant get a reduced price for his lunch at the expense of his often-but-not-always-wealthy landlord. Economist Steven Cheung reports that in 1921, the attorney general of Hong Kong proudly proclaimed about a new rent control law: "The object of the Bill is to protect tenants, not landlords."[20] The attorney general's 1921 comments match the intuition of many folks in 2021. Not much has changed in one hundred years.

Yet, if rent control actually gives tenants a free lunch, why do economists oppose it? Are they merely soulless creatures, as some critics of economics constantly allege? Are economists heartless sociopaths who want less affordable housing for the poor?

Before I answer that question, I will first provide some evidence that economists do, indeed, oppose rent control. Every few weeks, the University of Chicago's "Initiative on Global Markets" polls some fifty of the world's leading economists. In 2012, the poll asked about rent control. The economists were asked about whether rent control in San Francisco and New York had a positive effect on the quantity and quality of housing. Ninety-five percent of the respondents indicated that rent control reduces both the quantity and quality of housing.[21]

One reason for this overwhelming consensus is the long and sordid history of attempts to control prices. Economists place rent control within the general category of price controls, which rulers have attempted since time immemorial. Each time, price controls have failed to deliver a free lunch.

In their book *Forty Centuries of Wage and Price Controls*, Robert Schuettinger and Eamonn Butler document the long and colorful history of price controls.[22] For instance, King Hammurabi includes them in his famous "Code of Hammurabi," circa 2000 B.C. As Schuettinger and Butler document, we can find plenty of cases from ancient China, India, and Egypt.

In each case, the results were the same. Attempts to provide a free lunch effectively made the price system illegal for a certain range of prices. Because buyers and sellers can't bypass the price system, they're forced to resort to other, sometimes quite bizarre, ways of allocating goods.

To understand these alternative means of allocation, let's begin by looking at the interesting history of San Francisco housing. In 1906, a violent earthquake shook San Francisco for one minute. For the next three days, fires swept through the city. When the dust settled, half of San Francisco's housing units were gone.

Despite the devastation, Nobel Prize–winning economists George Stigler and Milton Friedman document in their classic essay "Roofs or Ceilings: The Current Housing Problem" that there was no San Francisco housing shortage in 1906.[23] That's because the price of housing rose dramatically. In response, people adjusted their living situation by moving in with family members to save on rent. The high price also stimulated a swift rebuilding effort in the city as outside contractors poured in. Prices were hard at work, doing their job of allocating scarce housing space.

By contrast, in 1946, San Francisco's municipal government imposed rent control in anticipation of an incoming wave of soldiers and immigrants. Rent control did something that one of the worst natural disasters in U.S. history couldn't do—it created a housing shortage. On the one hand, some people ditched their annoying roommates and started looking for housing on their own due to the reduced rent. On the other hand, some housing owners removed their units from the market because maintenance was no longer worth it at the rent-controlled price.

The upshot was that people who wanted housing couldn't find rooms to rent. This is remarkable because the ratio of people to housing units was three times greater in 1906 after the disaster than in 1946 after the population surge. Faced with a shortage and inability to raise prices, sellers must devise other means of allocating scarce housing space.

Paris: City of Ghouls

I want to show you four alternative ways that people use to allocate goods when the law bars them from using prices. Be sure to look through the opportunity cost lens. For the first two allocation methods, I want you to focus on the opportunity cost of buyers. For the following two methods, we'll take a look at sellers' opportunity costs.

To examine buyers' opportunities costs, let's explore the most common way of allocating scarce housing space under rent control. Using prices is so beneficial that the most common allocation method is simply to resort to the price system again. Only this time, it's a bit sneaky.

For instance, in New York City, it's common for landlords to charge "key money" for keys or furniture—accessories usually provided for free. If a Manhattan apartment's market price was fifty dollars in 1946 (yes, a realistic price for the era), rent control might have capped the price at forty dollars a month. Rent control prompted entrepreneurial landlords to respond by adding monthly "key money" of ten dollars. In essence, landlords were saying, "Sure, you can have legal title to the apartment for forty a month. If you'd like to experience the pleasure of stepping inside, you'll need to pony up an even fifty."

Often, the municipal government anticipates this adjustment by criminalizing key money. That only moves exchanges underground. Landlords begin asking for bribes from potential tenants in dark alleys.

Notice how the rent control has failed to reduce the actual cost of acquiring title to scarce apartment space. The price may be no lower than before once you account for the "key money." Lunch isn't free. Buyers still bear an opportunity cost to acquire an apartment. Sellers would prefer to charge "key money," but when they can't get away with that, they sometimes have to simply allocate the apartment to whoever is most tenacious in hunting for it.

This discussion brings us to the second way of allocating housing when prices are outlawed. Allow me to share a crazy story to motivate this principle. The setting is post–World War II Paris.

Like San Francisco or New York, Paris had reinvigorated its rent control laws shortly after the war, anticipating soldiers returning home.

The French economist Bertrand de Jouvenel describes the consequences in a beautiful little 1948 essay called "No Vacancies."[24] Newly returned French soldiers were looking for a place to live, but they couldn't find anyone willing to rent at the low prices. And who wants to put up with a roommate, even the most fastidious, when rent is so cheap?

The Parisian episode turned genuinely sordid. De Jouvenel reports that many French soldiers' wives began stalking the oldest, sickest Parisians they could find. They'd carefully observe their daily routines from a distance and then stalk them back to their residences. On the first day that a "stalker" noticed one of the elderly folks she was stalking had failed to show up to his favorite café at the usual time, she'd make a phone call to his apartment building and ask the manager to check the room of the old man on the assumption that he'd passed away.

If he had, bingo! Perhaps a room was now available?

What could cause these Parisians to act in such a creepy, undignified fashion? Rent control could. By generating a massive shortage, rent control ensured that no apartment remained vacant for hardly any time to speak of. If you wanted an apartment, you had to be first in line when one came open. In Paris, potential tenants weren't competing by offering higher prices. They were competing by sacrificing their dignity. That's a cost, too.

Think also about all the time these couples wasted searching for an apartment. The apartment-hunters were sacrificing other valuable goals they might want to pursue. And unlike when you pay a money price, no one directly derives a benefit from you bearing a search cost. It's sheer waste. Don't forget the harm brought to the elderly either, as desperate Parisians casually violated their privacy.

Once again, we see that lunch isn't free. You can't simply legislate opportunity cost out of existence. But that hasn't stopped many from trying.

No Kids Allowed

Let's turn now to a third means of allocating apartments. It's at this point that things turn truly sordid. When landlords can't select the tenants who'd be willing to pay them the most, they can sometimes resort to other means of choosing their tenants.

An example will help us see how this plays out. Take the baseline case of no rent control first. When there's no rent control, a landlord facing one hundred potential tenants for a single room will simply raise his price and let the space go to the highest bidder. Rent control eliminates that option.

How does the landlord pick among the one hundred applicants when rent control constrains him? He might select tenants based on his racial, sexual, or religious preferences. Why can't he act this way when there isn't any rent control? Actually, he can. But there's a high opportunity cost. He risks the apartment sitting empty when he discriminates against someone for an arbitrary reason. Without a shortage—induced by the rent control— there's not a long line of people wanting to rent. When our landlord acts like a bigot, he can expect less rental income as units lie empty.

Contrast that with the rent control case. When there's a housing shortage, the landlord can discriminate based on his distinctive tastes because another person will always want to rent. The queue for housing may be long and filled with eager potential tenants. What's more, the next person might have the skin color that he prefers. Under rent control, the landlord's not risking a vacancy by acting like a bigot.

Rent control, of course, doesn't make people racist, but it lowers the opportunity cost of behaving in a racist fashion. That isn't just theoretically solid speculation. We have good empirical support for this idea from the economist Sven Rydenfelt, who examined rent control in the Swedish housing market.[25]

Rydenfelt shows that couples with children had a more challenging time finding housing after governments imposed rent control. Apartments went to childless couples and to singles. All else equal, it's easier to have childless couples because they're not drawing on your walls with crayons. Since a landlord can have his pick of potential tenants, he tends to choose the easiest to house—which includes childless couples.

Bombs Away!

The fourth means of allocating without prices is, perhaps, the hardest to see without your economic eyeglasses. Landlords can simply let the housing quality adjust until it matches the new, lower price they're forced to charge.

In other words, rent control doesn't just lower the opportunity cost of landlords' discrimination; it also reduces the opportunity cost of being an overall bad steward of the apartment building. Under rent control, we often observe landlords delaying or even forgoing maintenance. In other words, sometimes the attempt to give tenants a free lunch only causes the size of their lunch to shrivel. Tenants pay less, but they also walk away with an empty stomach—to stick with our free lunch analogy.

Why can't the landlord ignore the maintenance to save upkeep costs when there's no rent control? Again, he could. But there's an opportunity cost to ignoring maintenance when there's no rent control. The landlord risks losing tenants to the well-maintained apartment across the street. Remember, there's no shortage without rent control. That means it's easier to find an apartment, and it's harder to find new tenants.

Rent control, though, creates a housing shortage by holding prices below their free-market levels. Under a shortage, even if the landlord's not that responsive to tenant demands, there's always a long line of people waiting for an apartment. Once again, he doesn't risk a long vacancy by forgoing maintenance.

Suppose the lock on your apartment door breaks. You put in a maintenance request. The landlord responds with something like, "Listen, buddy, if you're not happy here, I've got a hundred other folks who'd be happy to take your place tomorrow." And then he takes his good old sweet time. Your lock stays broken for a month. You'd better hope that inhabitants of your city respect private property rights.

Where rent control is particularly severe, landlords sometimes abandon the dwelling altogether, leaving a path of destruction in their wake. For example, when New York City implemented rent control, arson rates in apartment complexes increased—so heavy were landlords' losses from the price control.[26]

There are other cases of landlords disappearing only to assume a new identity in the Caribbean. For some, that's preferable to owning housing in a rent-controlled environment. Cut your losses. When landlords flee, maintenance becomes a thing of the past. This has even led to instances of the apartment building collapsing into a heap of uninhabitable rubble.

Economist Assar Lindbeck observed that rent control is "the most efficient technique presently known to destroy a city—except for bombing it."[27]

Inspired by Lindbeck's observation, economists Walter Block and Edgar Olsen edited a book titled *Rent Control: Myths and Realities* that includes pictures of demolished apartment buildings. They ask their readers to guess whether the ruins resulted from bombs or rent control—with answers provided at the end of the book.

I suppose it's not common for an author to instruct his readers to put down the book for a moment. But that's what I want you to do. Seriously, pause for a few minutes, so that you can google Block and Olsen's book that is now in the public domain and available as a free PDF.[28]

Test your own ability to distinguish between bomb damage and rent control.

You're back? Well, you get the point. On the basis of visual evidence alone, there's no good way of distinguishing between bombs and rent control.

I'd imagine the particularly impatient prefer bombs.

No Pets Allowed

Hopefully, you've gotten the message so far: Lunch isn't free.

Interestingly, sometimes politicians half understand this point. As a result, they pass a more sophisticated rent control ordinance that allows landlords to raise their rent by (say) 10 percent every time they get a new tenant. We could call this a "graduated rent increase scheme."

Politicians see this as the best of both worlds. Give tenants a free lunch, but don't drive landlords to adopt a new identity in the Caribbean. It turns out that this doesn't work, either. The graduated rent increase scheme only introduces conflict to the landlord-tenant relationship where it didn't exist before. Landlords now want a high turnover rate so that they can continue increasing their rents.

This type of rent control stipulation increases the landlord's opportunity cost of keeping tenants happy in their units. As a result, the law gives landlords an incentive to pack their leases with small print and enforce those terms stringently. For example, they might prohibit any pets. That's pretty common for lease agreements—but landlords don't consistently enforce them.

A few pages ago, we saw that rent control can cause landlords to adopt a "no kids allowed" posture. In this, they may direct their ire at pets. When you're trying to kick tenants out, the opportunity cost of not enforcing your "pet clause" can be high. The owner would be foregoing the chance to welcome a tenant to whom he could charge higher rent.

Under the graduated rent increase scheme, landlords even sometimes hire neighborhood children to snoop on tenants. Landlords want to determine if a tenant might be harboring a cat in violation of the lease agreement. If the kids can get photographic evidence, all the better. Upon discovering an infraction, landlords respond swiftly by kicking out the first tenant, replacing him, and increasing the rent.

Economist Steven Cheung, examining Hong Kong's experience with rent controls, noticed that landlords even went to extremes, such as removing windows during monsoon season, in an attempt to force tenants out.[29] This behavior is the opposite of what we tend to observe in a market without rent control.

After four millennia of experience with price controls, we ought to have learned something. You can lower the price on a good all you want, but that doesn't make the good "free"—in the economic sense. The fact that lunch isn't free is an economic law that was true in 2021 B.C., around the time Hammurabi declared price controls. It was true when Pareto squabbled with Schmoller in the 1800s. And it's still true today.

There's still a limited quantity of goods, and that quantity has to be allocated somehow. People will incur costs to acquire goods. Many of the non-monetary costs, such as time, are hidden, but that doesn't mean they don't exist. Our economic eyeglasses allow us to see these hidden costs.

So, no. Economists aren't heartless sociopaths who want to see poor tenants suffering. It's just that when it comes to allocating goods, such as apartment space, we understand that the free price system is preferable to under-the-table-bribes, willingness to wait in line, or outright discrimination.

A secondary conclusion is that we ought to judge policies based on their outcomes—not their intentions. That's because policies often alter the opportunity costs that people face. Do proponents of rent control want to encourage racist behavior and elder stalking? Of course not!

Looking only at intentions, while ignoring outcomes, can ensnare us in many economic lies. We'll explore them more thoroughly in the next chapter.

CHAPTER THREE

INTENTIONS GUARANTEE OUTCOMES

The best–laid schemes 'o Mice an' Men
Gang aft a-gley.

~ Robert Burns

The Cobra Effect

In the early twentieth century, British colonizers of India confronted a serious problem. Cobras were slithering through the streets, even peacefully inhabiting homes of the native population.

Picture this humorous scene: Austere British redcoats, repeatedly startled as they encountered these deadly pests in the crowded streets of Delhi. Nothing in their training had prepared them for this.

To reduce the number of cobras, the British quickly devised a plan. They started offering bounties for cobra tails. The scheme seemed ingenious.

It didn't take long for the number of tails being redeemed for payment to grow suspiciously large. Were there that many cobras in Delhi? Why did it seem that they were hardly making a dent in the snake population? What was going on?

The British soon discovered that some locals had turned entrepreneurial. "Cobra farms" had popped up all around the outskirts of Delhi. Unlike the British, the indigenous population didn't jump at the snakes. Natives were breeding cobras in large numbers, severing their tails, and then redeeming them for payment. I'm no biologist, but I'm confident snakes don't need their tails to reproduce.

Upon this finding, the British immediately disbanded the reward system. Now out of business, the breeders released their cobras back into the wild. Delhi's serpent population ballooned. The whole venture was a massive failure. Instead of reducing the cobra population, the British colonizers had increased it.[30]

I wish I could tell you this happened only once. But we know plenty of similar tales—no pun intended—that illustrate the same dynamics.

For example, historian Michael Vann documents an episode that occurred in 1902.[31] In the wake of the new germ theory of disease, the French colonizers of Vietnam began a campaign to eradicate Hanoi's large sewer rat population. Vann's archival work shows that even though this campaign killed over 20,000 rats a day, the plan failed to dent the rat population substantially. Relying on altruism didn't do the trick.

So, the French government appealed to self-interest by instituting a bounty on rat tails. Before long, locals— call them "entrepreneurs"—started rat-breeding farms throughout Hanoi.

Government officials put two and two together when they observed tailless rats roaming the streets. As a result, the French disbanded their program, and the rat farmers released their now-worthless rodents back into the city. The rat population exploded.

These stories illustrate a fundamental economic principle: The best, noblest intentions in the world aren't sufficient to guarantee good outcomes. Despite what's commonly believed, it's not merely a "lack of political will" that keeps people from achieving their goals.

Many times, it's something far more fundamental. What is this reality that scuttles the "best-laid plans of mice and men"?

It's critical to understand that virtually all public policies alter the relationship between costs and benefits. When the benefits of an action change relative to an action's opportunity cost, people's actions also change. And when people change their actions, they may do so in a way that works at cross-purposes with a public policy's noble intentions. If the British had intended to increase the cobra population, their policy would have been a resounding success. Alas, their goal was just the opposite.

This chapter will help you avoid the pitfalls that Nobel Prize–winning economist Douglass North and his co-authors refer to in their book, *The Economics of Public Issues*. They write, "There is a saying among economists that politicians believe all demand curves and supply curves are perfectly inelastic."[32] That's "economic-ese," but the meaning is easy enough to grasp.

My translation goes something like this: Politicians often behave as if buyers will be "unresponsive" when a policy changes the relationship between the costs and the benefits buyers face. Similarly, politicians also act as if sellers will be unresponsive to changes in the costs and benefits they face. Of course, you already know that's not true.

A few moments' reflection on your own behavior will show that when the cost of an activity rises relative to its benefits, you do less of that thing. Picture yourself at the grocery store buying steak. If you find out that the price is double of what you expected, how much will you buy? Probably less than you originally planned, or none at all. You might buy chicken instead.[33]

Consider another example of buyers. The 1991 luxury tax on yachts caused the wealthy in the United States to cut back on their yacht-buying.[34] That's costs changing relative to benefits. The tax changed the behavior of the rich to such an extent that the government paid more in unemployment benefits to former yacht workers than it collected in tax revenue.

On the other hand, when the benefits of an activity rise relative to its costs, you do more of the activity. For example, we observe that when the wages associated with white-collar jobs rise relative to blue-collar jobs, more people go to college. That's benefits rising relative to costs.

Understanding the examples in this chapter is easy. It only requires that you look through the opportunity cost lens because that will focus your attention on how opportunity costs are changing relative to benefits. These examples illustrate that good intentions can backfire if your policy alters the relationship between the benefits and the costs people face.

You can get the "Cobra Effect"[35] that we saw at the beginning of this chapter all over again—and often with deadly consequences.

Runway Horror

In their book *The New World of Economics*, Richard McKenzie and Gordon Tullock derive important lessons from a sobering tragedy.[36] They tell us the story of United

Airlines Flight 232. On July 19, 1989, this plane was flying from Denver to Chicago.

It never made its destination. Instead, it crash-landed in Sioux City, Iowa, after one of its engines failed. Astonishing video footage shows the plane somersaulting down the runway amidst balls of flame. Of the 296 passengers on board, 112 perished, including two infants.

In the wake of this horrific accident, two Republican representatives, Jim Lightfoot of Iowa and Kit Bond of Missouri, proposed new legislation. As McKenzie and Tullock describe it, the Lightfoot-Bond proposal would have required that parents strap infants and toddlers into safety seats on commercial planes.[37]

The rationale seemed sound. On Flight 232, the two infants tragically lost their lives because they were sitting on their mothers' laps. During the turbulent landing, they became loose and suffered severe head trauma.

Lightfoot and Bond's well-intentioned legislation would prevent this outcome by strapping children safely into a seat. The National Transportation Safety Board and the Los Angeles Area Child Passenger Safety Association—wow, that's a mouthful—threw their support behind the Lightfoot-Bond proposal. James Kolstad, chairman of the National Transportation Safety Board, proclaimed, "The economic cost of the extra passenger seat is a very small price for preventing injuries and saving lives."[38]

Did you catch the word Kolstad used? "Cost." The Lightfoot-Bond legislation would raise air travel costs relative to air travel benefits. The law means that travelers with infants must give up more to travel by air. The law would force parents traveling with a child to purchase an additional seat on the plane for their infant.

Why does that matter? How would this legislation likely lead to more—instead of fewer—infant fatalities? Remember that when the opportunity cost of an action rises relative to the benefits, some people will begin searching for substitute means of achieving their goals.

In this case, driving by car is the most common substitute for flying. Lightfoot argued, "The potential for injury in an aircraft flying at 550 miles per hour is much greater than the potential for injury in an automobile traveling at fifty miles per hour." That's true—if you only consider the speed and ignore the frequency of accidents. When we consider the risk of getting in an accident, the picture changes.

Cars are much more accident-prone than planes. In the U.S. during the 1980s, you were thirty-five times more likely to die in a car than on a plane when evaluated on a per-mile basis. Not to mention that the risk of permanent injury was also significantly higher in automobiles relative to planes.

Meanwhile, a Federal Aviation Administration (FAA) study showed that mandatory infant safety seats could have prevented at most one death during the ten years between

1978 and 1988. In stark contrast, almost 1,200 children under age five died in auto accidents in 1988 alone. The FAA further calculated that children's mandatory safety seats would increase the average cost of air travel by at least 21 percent for a family of four.

Of course, we can't know how many travelers that cost increase would send to the roads. But we know it would send some since the costs of flying would have risen relative to the benefits. That's just this chapter's principle. People's actions change when costs change relative to benefits.

For their part, the FAA estimated the Lightfoot-Bond proposal would reduce the number of infants flying in the U.S. by about 700,000 annually. Of those, many would be hitting the roads instead. From the perspective of infant safety, here's the good news: the Lightfoot-Bond proposal never passed.

Its failure to become law certainly saved lives. I confidently make that claim because we have good empirical evidence about what happens when flying becomes more costly. The 9/11 attacks raised the cost of flying by increasing the time people spent waiting in airport security, and there's an opportunity cost of waiting in line. In Chapter One, we examined the devastation of the 9/11 attacks. But the results of the terrorists' dreadful actions weren't confined to that horrific day alone.

McKenzie and Tullock cite economists Garrick Blalock, Vrinda Kadiyali, and Daniel Simon who estimate that, due to these increased costs of flying, 327 additional automobile deaths occurred monthly for the last quarter of 2001.[39] Overall, Blalock and his coauthors attribute 2,300 additional American deaths to road fatalities that occurred because of the attacks and the subsequent public policy response. We'll never know how much terrorist activity the security response to 9/11 prevented, but this much is sure—there were certainly other fatalities stemming from the activities of the TSA.

Making air travel more costly encourages people to use more dangerous substitutes. Once again, we see the lesson: Intentions don't guarantee outcomes.

Ban-the-Box

Plenty of public policies have great intentions. Like the legislation we just examined, the following policy fails to achieve its stated goal and even worsens outcomes for the very people the policymakers are trying to help. Just like the preceding examples, we observe this result because the policy changes buyers' costs relative to benefits.

In the United States, roughly 637,000 people are released from prison each year.

Unsurprisingly, it's often challenging for these individuals to find work. This is true even when we compare them to people who have similar education and work experience—

NO FREE LUNCH ● CALEB S. FULLER

but have no criminal record. Ex-convicts are perceived as (and are) riskier hires.

Some U.S. jurisdictions have introduced something called "ban-the-box" legislation to aid these disenfranchised job-seekers. As of late 2017, thirty-four U.S. states had at least one jurisdiction with a ban-the-box law, or "BTB" for short. A BTB law prevents employers from asking prospective employees about their criminal history until very late in the hiring process. The curious name comes from the little box on a job application form that anyone with a criminal record would mark. BTB prevents employers from including that box on job applications.

Proponents of the law reason that if employers can't distinguish between those with records and those without them, former criminals will receive interview offers more readily. For BTB advocates, the thinking goes like this: Once an ex-convict gets an interview, he can reveal his criminal record, but he also now has a chance to demonstrate his qualifications for the job.

But this policy does nothing to alter the job-readiness of former criminals. Employers are still wary of hiring a former convict who turns out to be a bad apple.

Economists Jennifer Doleac and Benjamin Hansen describe this suspicion in a 2020 paper.[40] Doleac and Hansen comment, "A criminal background is still linked to less preparedness for many jobs. When BTB removes information about a criminal record from job applications, employers may respond by using the remaining observable information to try to guess who ex-offenders are and avoid interviewing them."

Doleac and Hansen uncover empirical evidence that BTB laws do encourage employers to "guess" who the ex-offenders are. In fact, they find that Hispanic and African American men are less likely to receive interviews after a jurisdiction passes BTB. With fewer interviews, these men also receive fewer job offers.

Why? Young, low-skilled, Hispanic, and African American men are statistically more likely to have a criminal record than other U.S. groups. Employers' behavior indicates that they are aware of this statistic.

Where jurisdictions impose BTB, Hispanic and African American male employment plummets relative to jurisdictions without the law. On average, BTB laws reduced employment for African American men by 3.4 percentage points. They reduced employment by 2.3 percentage points for young Hispanic men. And where these populations are less numerous, such as the American Northeast, the effects have been even more dramatic.

In contrast to these results, there's no statistically discernible influence of BTB on young white males' employment prospects.

BTB increases the costs of learning who has a criminal record. It's costly for an employer to pursue a job-seeker to the end of the hiring process, only to discover the applicant has a criminal record. So, rather than incur the costs associated with searching, some employers go to the next-best and lower-opportunity-cost source of information. That happens to be a person's racial or demographic characteristics. African American and Hispanic men are more likely to have a criminal record than Caucasian men. As a result, they receive interview offers less frequently.

"Ban-the-box" has excellent intentions, of course. But it decreases the likelihood that minorities find employment.

DIY

I want to conclude with one more sobering example. Death rates by electrocution, poor dental hygiene, and blindness aren't evenly distributed across the U.S. population. How would you explain these facts?

If you're wearing your economic eyeglasses, you'll start by guessing that the opportunity costs of hiring electricians, dentists, and optometrists differ from region to region.

That's precisely the case.

In the United States, roughly a quarter of all workers are subject to an occupational licensing law.[41] These laws require that would-be sellers pay fees to the government or pass a battery of government-mandated exams before they can begin operating legally. As a result, licenses tend to reduce the number of sellers operating in a given market. Licensing increases the cost of becoming a seller. Due to the license, potential sellers must now jump through hoops to become legal. Some wannabe sellers decide the cost of those hoops is prohibitive. They decide not to enter the market at all.

While the stated rationale of licensing laws is always to protect the consumer, it's unclear exactly how a required class in advanced hydrology—which some states require plumbers to pass—does anything other than decrease the supply of plumbers. It's also unclear how occupational licensing for psychics—which jurisdictions such as Annapolis, Maryland, have—is supposed to protect consumers from charlatans and quacks.[42]

When you restrict the supply of something, you raise its price. And when you raise the price of something, many buyers will search for cheaper substitutes. We already saw that with the airplane safety seat legislation.

If you're looking through the opportunity cost lens, you've probably already guessed the answer to our puzzle. Economists Sidney Carroll and Robert Gaston have empirically demonstrated that states with the most deaths by electrocution, the worst dental hygiene, and the most blindness are also the states with the most stringent occupational licensing of electricians, dentists, and optometrists, respectively.[43] What a coincidence!

Some homeowners judge the opportunity cost of hiring a professional electrician to be prohibitively high. Tragically, for some of these individuals, a DIY YouTube video is their substitute for an artificially high-priced professional electrician.

Notice how our economic eyeglasses enable us to gain a clearer picture of grim statistics like this one. Without our eyeglasses, all we see is a fateful accident that we attribute merely to insufficient caution or overconfidence in one's skills. Those things may be true, but they're not the full story. However, with our economic eyeglasses, we understand how this accident resulted from the inflated price for electricians.

Think about how perverse that outcome is from the perspective of the politicians who supported the occupational licensing law. Their intention was undoubtedly to prevent unqualified people from messing around with electrical wires. But this law brought about more of the very thing they were seeking to avoid. More unqualified people messing around with wires. Instead of reducing the risk of death by electrocution, well-meaning politicians increased it.

A large number of economists oppose occupational licensing.[44] In fact, I think consumers would be better off if licensing were abolished altogether. Many economists share my view. That belief is so common among economists due to what I consider the most critical insight in economics. We'll examine that lesson in the next chapter. And if you're wondering what happens to quality in a world without licensing, well, read to the end of the book.

CHAPTER FOUR

EXCHANGE IS EXPLOITATION

I'll give you five dollars for three more M&M's.

~ My nephew, Matthias, age 3

The Most Important Lesson

I concluded our previous chapter with a provocative claim: abolishing occupational licensing laws would improve consumer welfare. In this chapter, I'll explain the main reason I made that claim.

Recall that licensure reduces the supply of workers in the licensed field. That reduction raises the wages of licensed workers. But, as we saw in the last chapter, fewer people then make exchanges with them. Why, then, do I think consumers would be better off if we abolished all licensing laws?

In short, because licensing laws reduce the number of mutually beneficial exchanges that people make. A fundamental tenet of economics is that all voluntary exchanges are beneficial to both parties. At least that's the trading partners' expectation before the exchange occurs.

Don't just take my word for it. Writing in 2001, the 1986 winner of the Nobel Prize in Economics, James Buchanan, states, "The mutuality of advantage from voluntary exchange is the most fundamental of all understandings in economics."[45]

Along similar lines, the great twentieth-century economist Ludwig von Mises writes in his 1949 magnum opus, *Human Action*, "The exchange relation is the fundamental social relation. Interpersonal exchange of goods and services weaves the bond which unites men into society."[46]

The reason for economists' confidence that all exchange benefits both parties hinges on a single word that appeared in the Buchanan quote: "Voluntary." When an exchange is voluntary, neither party brings violence or the threat of violence to the negotiations. Both parties can either go through with the trade or retain title to their property. They are free to choose. This implies that no one would make a voluntary exchange unless he believes that what he'll gain from exchanging is more valuable than what he'll give up, that is, his opportunity cost.

When you shop at the grocery store, you may prefer having a bag of apples to having five dollars. Meanwhile, the store owner may prefer having the five dollars to having the bag of apples. In other words, people don't value goods identically, and when these "reverse valuations" exist, both parties will be better off if they exchange.

Likewise, you demonstrate that you value your paycheck more than whatever else you could be doing instead when you work a job. Your pay at least covers your opportunity cost of working. Your employer likewise values your labor services more than the money he pays you.

Thus, every trade makes the world wealthier because both parties gain, even as the exchange only switches who owns what property titles.

In other words, exchange fundamentally just moves "stuff" around. Even though the same amount of "stuff" exists before and after the exchange, it still makes us richer. When I trade away what I value less and replace it with what I cherish more, I become richer. So does my exchange partner. Pretty amazing.

Of course, I don't deny the familiar phenomenon of "buyer's remorse." You can come to rue an exchange afterward. The claim is that, before exchange takes place, both parties anticipate they'll benefit. If that weren't the case, one or both parties would refuse to interact. Since we're only considering voluntary exchanges, if even one of the buyers didn't anticipate gain, nothing would happen; no exchange would occur.

That's it. That's this chapter's lesson.

Yet, the implications are far-reaching and sometimes challenging to see without well-calibrated economic eyeglasses. That trade makes both parties better off is a seemingly commonsensical insight to some people. Nonetheless, throughout history, many thinkers have devoted significant intellectual energy to denying this very insight.

In many instances, the idea that exchange is mutually beneficial has eluded even the world's brightest minds. Aristotle, for example, thought people exchanged when both parties valued the goods equally. In his understanding, exchange doesn't make people worse off, but it doesn't make them better off, either. As we saw a moment ago, Aristotle's view is flawed because people exchange when they each believe they'll be made better off from trading. If not, why exchange?

Another tremendous intellect, medieval theologian Thomas Aquinas, believed that many voluntary exchanges were, indeed, mutually beneficial—but that not all were. Aquinas maintained that exchanges occurring at exceptionally high prices were nothing short of theft by sellers. In his view, one party can benefit from voluntary trade while the other party loses.

These and similar misconceptions thrive even today. Giants such as Aristotle and Aquinas wrote before the advent of economics. Modern intellectuals have no such excuse. Today, someone holding that exchange is exploitation is clinging to a lie.

Such lies provide the intellectual firepower for the idea that individuals would be better off if the government restricts exchange in certain instances. Historically, the most common argument for restricting some trades is that not all voluntary exchanges are mutually beneficial. As we just saw, many thinkers, like Aquinas, have held that voluntary exchange benefits one party while harming the other. This perspective on exchange sees trade as fundamentally "zero-sum"—one man's gain is another man's loss.

In this view, the essence of exchange is exploitation. For this chapter, "exploitation" refers to an interaction that leaves one party worse off than before the exchange. If you read the free online *Stanford Encyclopedia of Philosophy*'s entry on "exploitation," you'll see that this is an everyday use of the term, though admittedly not its only use.[47]

The view that voluntary exchange can be exploitative, in this sense, is expressed well by the sixteenth-century French philosopher Michel de Montaigne. In one of his famous essays, published in 1580, Montaigne wrote, "No profit whatever can possibly be made but at the expense of another."[48] Montaigne elaborates on this comment by arguing that doctors exploit the fact that people become ill, while architects exploit the fact that our buildings continually crumble.

To an economist, those claims don't hold water. Here's how economist Ludwig von Mises responds to Montaigne.

He writes in *Human Action*, "What produces a man's profit ...is not his fellow citizen's plight and distress..." and now, the linchpin of Mises' argument: "but the fact that he alleviates or entirely removes what causes his fellow citizen's feeling of uneasiness. What hurts the sick is the plague, not the physician who treats the disease. The doctor's gain is not an outcome of the epidemics, but of the aid he gives to those affected."[49]

I think many people do accept Mises' argument for most exchanges. Still, you might wonder about "hard cases" that seem—at least on the surface—to be genuinely exploitative. Is it true that all voluntary exchanges are mutually beneficial? This question is important because the lie that "exchange is exploitation" supports public policies that harm the very people they're intended to help.

Head, Not Heart

Once again, we must look through the opportunity cost lens to see how even seemingly lopsided exchanges are mutually beneficial.

Let's be concrete. What about people living in the underdeveloped world, working jobs that pay low wages and offer poor conditions by Western standards? Can we say that those individuals benefit from exchanging their labor with their employers? Alternatively, are they exploited and therefore made worse off?

If these workers are exploited, could we make them better off by creating public policies that punish their employers for the exploitation? Could we benefit these workers by banning imports of goods that low-wage laborers in the underdeveloped world manufacture?

To answer that policy question, we first need to examine whether these workers are exploited or if they benefit from their work. Again, remember my definition of exploitation: One party harms the other.

Let me be crystal clear about the sorts of situations I have in mind. I'm not referring to enterprises that use coerced or slave labor. Those situations are clearly tragic and truly exploitative because the laborers are not voluntarily choosing their situation. I'm only referring to enterprises in the underdeveloped world that mostly pay low wages, typically expect long hours, and usually provide poor working conditions. The key is that all employees in these situations are working from their free initiative. There is no coercion involved in the cases I'm thinking of.

Do the employers in these contexts benefit at the laborers' expense? According to many commentators in the Western world, this is undoubtedly an exploitative exchange.

What does the opportunity cost lens suggest, however? It shows us that as long as the employees work voluntarily, they benefit from exchanging their labor for their employer's low wages. How does exchanging one's labor for a low wage benefit workers in underdeveloped nations? In a nutshell, it's because low-wage factory employment is superior to the relevant alternatives that confront these workers. You probably guessed it, but just so that we're on the same page, a "relevant alternative" is your best foregone option.

Now let's unpack the idea that low-wage factory employment is superior to the relevant alternatives for millions of the world's poorest people. It's easy to confuse the notion of "better off" with "well off." Looking through the opportunity cost lens fixes this error. By the standards of the developed world, the workers we're discussing are not "well off." Even the relatively poor in developed countries live materially comfortable lives relative to someone working twelve-hour days, six days a week in a Bangladeshi factory for one dollar an hour.

Reflect, for a moment, on what I'm claiming. The economic theory of exchange only says that exchange makes people "better off"—not that it makes them instantaneously wealthy, solves all their problems, or makes them "well off" in some objective sense. The fact that even a low-wage factory worker is made "better off" from exchange suggests that this laborer's relevant alternatives are not very enticing.

Economist Benjamin Powell has done the empirical work to document those relevant alternatives in his 2014 book, *Out of Poverty: Sweatshops in the Global Economy.*[50]

Powell shows that in such countries as Bangladesh, Cambodia, Haiti, Laos, and Vietnam, more than 40 percent of the population lives on less than two dollars a day. By contrast to that abysmal figure, Powell finds that the average factory worker earns ten dollars a day in those countries. This is terrible by Western standards, but it is significantly better than average wages in those countries.

These wage differences make it easy to see why an employee benefits from a low-paying factory job relative to the alternative of even lower-paying jobs. What about working conditions in these sorts of factories? After all, many concerns about labor in the underdeveloped world arise from the working conditions rather than the pay.

Unsurprisingly, working conditions are also bad by Western standards. Hours are long, and working conditions are much more dangerous than they are in Western factories. The critical question, though, is how these conditions compare to workers' relevant alternatives. To answer that question, Powell and his co-author, economist J.R. Clark, surveyed Guatemalan textile factory employees about their working conditions.[51]

Powell and Clark ask employees if they'd be willing to trade some of their wages to improve different features of their work environment. This is a helpful question because it gives us even deeper insight into these workers' relevant alternatives. The results may shock those of us who have very good relevant alternatives. Powell and Clark find that 95.7 percent of the low-income employees say they wouldn't trade any income for safer conditions. Over 95 percent also say they wouldn't trade any income for more extended bathroom or lunch breaks.

Importantly for our question about relevant alternatives, Powell and Clark also find that most employees say that their textile manufacturing jobs are safer and pay higher wages than their previous jobs. Moreover, an astonishing 100 percent of respondents report that their factory jobs offer more benefits than their last jobs did. It's little wonder, then, that employees sign up for these jobs. It makes them better off relative to their relevant alternative, which is not to say that they're "well off"—only "better off."

If you find yourself reasoning, "I'd never accept a position with those working conditions, so this must be exploitation!" you can discover the error in your thinking by looking through the opportunity cost lens. What would you give up if you took this job? What's your opportunity cost? Your relevant alternative might be a high-paying job in an air-conditioned office. Or it might be investing in your education by purchasing additional years of school. It could even be that you're sufficiently wealthy that you'd simply enjoy more leisure time.

What is the relevant alternative for someone who takes a low-paying factory job in the underdeveloped world? The relevant alternative is an even lower-paying and even more dangerous job, such as those found in agriculture or illicit work. Think prostitution and drugs. People work factory jobs in the underdeveloped world because it's their least-bad option of the bad options they face. Relevant alternatives pay less or are more dangerous, or both.

Therefore, it makes little sense to blame these employers for offering something better than anyone else is offering to these workers. Speaking personally for a moment, I've never extended these workers any wage, so I'm not going to condemn a large company that offers them something.

Recognizing that voluntary exchange is always mutually beneficial has important policy implications if our goal is to benefit the least well-off on our planet. The most important implication is that we can't make the least well-off better off by impeding their ability to exchange with employers, even low-paying employers.

More generally, workers are often in bad situations because they have few alternatives. You can't improve their standing by removing one of their bad options—especially when that's the option they've chosen.

Doing so can have deadly consequences for those in the underdeveloped world. Therefore, the opportunity cost lens tells us that certain public policies aimed at helping workers in underdeveloped countries may harm those workers instead. Think back to what we discussed in the last chapter. Intentions don't guarantee outcomes.

NO FREE LUNCH ● CALEB S. FULLER

Unfortunately, many developed nations have passed laws prohibiting the importation of items produced by factory workers in the world's poorest countries. Similarly, many private groups have organized grassroots boycotts of companies known for paying low wages and supplying poor working conditions.

Both attempts to punish employers worsen the plight of the world's poorest people. These policies ultimately reduce the demand for factory workers, which causes some of them to take a pay cut. Worse yet, others lose their jobs altogether along with their primary income stream.

Where do the newly unemployed workers end up? Think back to their relevant alternatives. They end up in other sectors that offer lower pay or more dangerous working conditions, such as agriculture, self-employment, or illegal activities. The bottom line is that poorly paid factory workers benefit from their employment, even if that benefit is not as great as we'd ultimately like to see. Exchange isn't exploitation.

Thus, even left-leaning economists such as Paul Krugman—who we saw in our opening chapter—or Oxford economist Paul Collier oppose policies that would punish large multinational employers of impoverished workers. At the risk of stating the obvious, Krugman and Collier's opposition to such policies as an import ban isn't because they're in love with large corporations. It's because they believe these policies will cause harm to the world's poorest people.

As I said in Chapter One, economics is true, regardless of your preferred ideology.

At this point, you might have many other questions. For example, you might be wondering why workers in the underdeveloped world don't command higher wages or why large manufacturing companies can't simply pay their poor workers even more than they do. Those are good questions, and economics does have answers for them, but they're also beyond the scope of this short book.

That said, I do want to leave this chapter on an optimistic note. One piece of good news is that economic development eventually eliminates low-paying and dangerous manufacturing work. Wherever economic growth occurs, workers' wages and working conditions swiftly rise until they become comparable to those in the wealthiest nations.

Thankfully, the process of economic development has been lifting countless millions worldwide out of poverty for the last two centuries or so. The number of people living in what the World Bank calls "extreme poverty" (living on less than $1.90 a day) has fallen from 1.9 billion in 1990— the year of my birth—to 650 million in 2018. As tens of millions exit grinding subsistence, they also leave behind low wages and undesirable working conditions.[52]

For those of us who care about the welfare of the world's poorest, that's something to celebrate. In the meantime, let's not get in the way of that development process by supporting laws that unintentionally harm the world's poorest people. If you hadn't already learned the lesson from Chapter Three, here it is one more time with feeling: Let's think with our heads, not our hearts.

Cut Out the Middleman?

There's another example that people raise as an exception to the argument that exchange is always mutually beneficial. This one is less emotionally charged than my previous example, but even more people might hold to this lie.

Do middlemen exploit us? People exchange with middlemen—such as stockbrokers, real estate agents, wholesalers, and even romantic matchmakers—all the time. Precisely what services do middlemen provide? Are they just leeches? It certainly doesn't seem that they're producing anything from a physical standpoint. Are they an exception to our principle that exchange makes both parties better off? Once again, many people think so.

To an economist, though, the claim is strange. Frederic Bastiat comments on middlemen in the same essay that gave us the broken window story that we saw in our first chapter. He writes, "[Some] ...are vehement in their attack on those they call middlemen, accusing [middlemen] of interposing themselves between producer and consumer, in order to fleece them both, without giving them anything of value."[53]

Bastiat is poetically explaining the intuitions many people share. Their instinct suggests that middlemen have devised a way of rudely inserting themselves into transactions where they have no legitimate business to exploit the other parties exchanging.

Indeed, many people believe that middlemen live at the expense of their exchange partners, all while providing no value to them in return—they're simply parasites on otherwise value-creating interactions. I remember a lunch hour at my first job after college where a coworker passionately held forth on how banks, real estate agents, and other middlemen are nothing but a drag on the economy.

To see what service the middleman is providing, we must put on our economic eyeglasses. Notice that part of making a successful exchange means searching for and identifying an exchange partner.

Our exchange partners don't just fall from the heavens. It might seem obvious, but failure to internalize this fact lurks behind the middleman-as-exploiter lie. Further, our search for exchange partners consumes real resources, such as our time. In other words, searching for exchange partners comes with an opportunity cost.

Middlemen reduce these costs by collecting knowledge about who would like to buy, who would like to sell, and at what prices. By providing this service, middlemen lower

NO FREE LUNCH ■ CALEB S. FULLER

the total costs that exchange partners bear—even when the middleman has the gall to demand compensation for the services he's rendered. People still anticipate gain from using a middleman compared to their relevant alternative of going it alone. Hence, their willingness to exchange with them.

You can make this more concrete by considering the following scenario. Imagine a college student who owns shares of Apple stock that he wishes to sell. Without middlemen—in this case, stockbrokers—who specialize in bringing stock buyers together with stock sellers, he'd be stuck knocking on dorm rooms until he found a buyer.[54] Think about the opportunity cost of his time. And what are the odds that he'd find the buyer willing to pay him the highest price for the stock? Probably pretty low. In the end, the college student benefits from exchanging with a middleman stockbroker.

We can apply the same reasoning to middlemen in every other context. Our logic explains why homes sell faster when a real estate agent is working the case, for instance. Thus, it simply doesn't make sense to mindlessly repeat the mantra about "cutting out the middleman."

In this chapter, we learned that the root of the exploitation lie is a failure to consider the relevant alternatives exchanging parties face. Implicitly, a person arguing that exchange is exploitation is saying something like this: "Suppose a person isn't sick, suppose a laborer *doesn't* live in a poor country, and suppose the college student *already* knows who wants to pay the highest price for his stock."

Sure, if those things were true, then it's hard to see how the exchanges discussed above would be anything short of exploitation.

In our world, the real world, people do get sick, they do live in underdeveloped countries, and they are ignorant of potential exchange partners.

Remember the quote from Mises at the beginning of this chapter. The fact that we live in this "vale of tears" means that we do benefit from exchanging with doctors, who save us from sickness.

Workers in the underdeveloped world do benefit from exchanging their labor with large corporations who rescue the worker from a worse fate and lessen the worker's poverty in the process—even if they don't eliminate it.

We do benefit from exchanging with stockbrokers, who eliminate our ignorance of exchange opportunities.

Arguments against voluntary exchange come from a fantasy world, not from the real world where people face concrete trade-offs.

In this chapter, we focused on a simple yet often misunderstood lesson: If exchange is voluntary, it's not exploitation. Both parties expect to benefit, everywhere and always.

In the next chapter, we'll address another challenge posed to the idea that free exchange benefits society's members. This objection questions whether the basic principles of exchange explained in this chapter hold when we start drawing political boundaries on the map. It's to those doubts that we'll turn to in Chapter Five.

TRADE IS WAR

If goods don't cross borders, armies will.

~ Otto T. Mallery[55]

Economists Agree

In the last chapter, we examined the erroneous argument that some voluntary trades impose harm systematically on one of the parties. We saw that this view is particularly destructive when it leads governments to restrict exchange with those in the underdeveloped world.

There's a second argument for why restricting voluntary exchanges could benefit society. This objection is a close cousin of the argument we examined in the last chapter. However, this objection accepts the idea that voluntary exchange isn't exploitation. Instead, it argues that something about trade changes when we draw a political line in the proverbial sand.

The objection goes like this. Is it possible that allowing free international trade could cause our society to become poorer? After all, can't we protect domestic employment if we prevent exchange with foreigners? If we decrease trade with foreigners, surely we'll strengthen domestic production. What's not to like? Perhaps voluntary exchanges don't make our society wealthier after all.

This view frequently describes international trade using military metaphors. For instance, trade with China is described as "warfare." Those subscribing to this view see the United States as "losing" in its trade relations with China. Similarly, adherents of this position advocate returning to a "fair" trading relationship with China or other nations. In this view, "fairness" usually involves public policies that protect our domestic industries from foreign competition. To sum it up, this lie holds that our international trading partners are "stealing" our jobs and making us poorer in the process. Trade is war.

The conclusion is that we could make ourselves better off by restricting the number of Chinese goods that we consume. The preferred policy to achieve this outcome is almost always tariffs, which are just taxes on goods produced by foreigners. Such tariffs make it less profitable for foreigners to sell in our country, which means domestic purchases and employment will rise. Or so the argument goes.

If you find that conclusion compelling, you might be surprised to learn that few policy issues garner as much consensus among economists as does their belief that tariffs don't make our society—or any society—wealthier, on the whole.

Before I give you that evidence, a few quick caveats: Governments have to raise money somehow. Our discussion doesn't concern the best way for a government to acquire funds. Here, we're also not interested in other arguments for tariffs, such as whether they're essential to national defense. Instead, we're interested in the more fundamental question of whether a tariff is a suitable policy tool for increasing a nation's wealth. Economists answer with a resounding and unanimous "no"!

In 2018, the University of Chicago's "Initiative on Global Markets" poll asked roughly fifty leading economists to respond to the following statement: "Imposing new U.S. tariffs on steel and aluminum will improve Americans' welfare." Not a single economist agreed with that statement. Twenty-four percent of them merely "disagreed," while the other seventy-six percent "strongly disagreed."[56]

What explains this opposition to tariffs? Or, to put it more positively, what's the case for free trade? We'll examine the second question first. Then we'll come back to how tariffs make our society poorer on the whole.

The World's Best Drummer

By this point, you shouldn't be surprised by how economists ground their thinking about international trade. Seeing how free international trade makes us wealthier requires you to look through the opportunity cost lens. In a nutshell, the opportunity cost lens shows that even when Tom is more productive than Bill, Tom still benefits from specializing and then exchanging with Bill. The same holds at the country level. That's an abstract principle, but it's easy to grasp with a few concrete examples. We'll start at the individual level and work our way up to the level of society.

Economist Kenneth Boulding offers a classic example in his text *Economic Analysis*: "A doctor who is an excellent gardener may very well prefer to employ a hired man, who, as a gardener is inferior to himself, because thereby he can devote more time to his medical practice."[57]

What's Boulding driving at? When a brain surgeon tends to his garden, he sacrifices the chance to use that time to perform brain surgeries, for which he charges a hefty sum. That hefty sum becomes his opportunity cost when he's gardening. If our brain surgeon wants to maximize his income, it may make sense for him to pay a gardener—even if the doctor has more of a green thumb than the gardener himself. This arrangement makes the rest of society better off, too. After all, we gain from this doctor conducting life-saving surgeries.

I like to illustrate this principle to my students with a debunked witticism that was attributed to the Beatles' John Lennon. A reporter asked Lennon if Ringo was the best drummer in the world. Lennon replied: "He's not even the best drummer in the Beatles!"

This conversation never happened, but some lies are useful (not economic lies, of course). Even if Ringo wasn't the best drummer in the Beatles, it still might make sense for Ringo to find himself on the drums. The Beatles would sacrifice incalculably by putting John, Paul, or George on the drums. They simply wouldn't be the Beatles anymore.

Likewise, if our brain surgeon spends all of his time in the garden simply because he's better than the local gardener, we wouldn't get brain surgeries anymore.

Applying these examples to international trade is instructive. People in the United States benefit from exchanging with people in China—even though the average American worker is more productive than the average Chinese laborer. In the example I just gave, "Americans" are the proverbial "brain surgeon." It is not because of any inherent difference between the two groups, but only because Americans have better machines and a better institutional environment.

When people in the United States buy steel from Chinese producers, U.S. workers don't have to devote their labor and resources to steel production. Instead, they can commit it to something else, say, programming computers or growing wheat, two things that Americans are very good at producing. Thus, when Americans trade with the Chinese, there is more steel, more tech, and more wheat for citizens in both countries to enjoy. It's just like the case where our brain surgeon trades with the gardener.

Meet the Lykovs

If you're still not convinced, consider another of my favorite illustrations for showing how unrestricted trade makes us wealthier. First, think of a family instead of a country. Suppose it's the hypothetical Smith family. The Smith family's father gets it in his head that the Smiths will be better off if they buy local only. As in, really local. Perhaps they should buy only from another family member. That way, no income ever leaves the family.

He also spots what he thinks is an added benefit: Everyone in the family will always have a job. There will be more than enough work to ensure that no one is idle. To secure these benefits, he decides to forbid exchanges with anyone outside the immediate Smith family.

We might call this dad a tyrant, but that's beside the point from an economic perspective. What else can we say using the opportunity cost lens? It won't take long for this family to become incredibly poor. If they're sick, they can't exchange with a doctor. They have to produce medicine themselves. If they want more clothes, they'd better learn to be content with what they can make on their own.

Want an education? Forget that. The Smith family will have to independently rediscover any knowledge they seek because they can't exchange for a teacher's services. Does anyone think they'll rediscover the fundamental theorem of calculus?

Interestingly, my example isn't pure conjecture. We have empirical evidence of what happens when a family gets cut off from all exchange opportunities. In the early twentieth century, a Russian family of six called the Lykovs fled their tiny town of Lykovo to escape the religious persecution seeking to exterminate adherents of the Russian Orthodox faith. They ended up in south Siberia, where they remained isolated for forty-two years—until a team of geologists stumbled on them in 1978.

When this team of scientists found the Lykovs, they were in terrible health, living in a small cabin with tattered clothes. Their diet consisted of only three or four different foods. They had never heard of World War II. That's what happens to your living standard when you can't exchange.[58]

Trade is the primary means by which humans cope with the scarcity of resources that we saw in Chapter Two. Without exchange, scarcity dooms the human race to grinding poverty. Exchange, by contrast, opens the door to material prosperity.

Apply this same logic, this same intuition, to the United States. In essence, we're just one big—and largely unhappy—family. We wouldn't be as poor as the Lykovs if we stopped exchanging with people in other countries, but we'd be poorer than if we did.

It's for this reason that Adam Smith remarks in his 1776 book, *An Inquiry into the Nature and Causes of the Wealth of*

Nations: "What is prudence in the conduct of every private family can scarce be folly in that of a great kingdom. If a foreign country can supply us with a commodity cheaper than we ourselves can make it, better to buy it of them with some part of the produce of our own industry."[59] That's just the logic of the brain surgeon and the gardener once again.

Trade Is Magic

Economist Steven Landsburg tells the second story I want to share about the benefits of international trade.[60] They ask us to imagine an eccentric billionaire inventor—an Elon Musk figure—who makes a startling announcement. The entrepreneur proclaims he's invented a machine that can produce cars, using only a little labor and another ingredient. That's crazy on its own, but it gets even more fantastic when our inventor says that the only other input he needs is wheat.

No one believes him. No one, that is, until he starts ordering thousands of tons of wheat from Kansas farmers. The wheat gets shipped to his West Coast factory. To everyone's amazement, cars begin rolling off the assembly line only a few weeks after the first wheat shipments arrive.

Secrecy surrounds the entrepreneur's operations. Except for a few workers who've signed non-disclosure agreements, no one is allowed into his factory to see the magical wheat-to-cars machine.

CHAPTER FIVE: **TRADE IS WAR**

The average American is elated. The crazy entrepreneur's cars are higher quality, get better gas mileage, and are cheaper than Detroit's vehicles. Not only are car buyers thrilled, but Kansas wheat farmers are ecstatic due to the new demand. The only folks who don't love it are the Detroit automakers, who see a predictable slump in sales.

Finally, curiosity gets the better of an investigative journalist. He sneaks into the factory to get a peek at the machine. To his amazement, he finds the building empty. He walks to the back of the massive structure he'd taken to be a factory just moments ago. Another door opens up onto a loading dock. What does he see? Wheat being loaded onto giant ships.

The ships are making their way to Japan, where the entrepreneur trades the grain for Toyotas and Hondas. He loads these onto the vessel in place of the grain it had been carrying. Once the vessel has arrived in the states, the entrepreneur unloads it and sells the cars to eager American buyers.

When our mischievous journalist publishes his report, many Americans are outraged that the Japanese are putting Detroit automakers out of a job. In a fit of protectionist fury, they sweep a pro-tariff candidate into the presidency, a man who promises to make trade with Japan "fair," a man who promises that we'll stop "losing" in our trade relationships—a man who promises a so-called trade war.

What's the moral of this story? If Americans loved the new cars when they thought they were coming from a magical machine, they ought to still be thrilled even when their fantasies come crashing down. Likewise, international trade should thrill us just as much as the magical wheat-to-cars machine. In other words, trade is another technology for producing the things we want. Trade is magic.

That's the basic argument for why free trade makes the world wealthier. In a nutshell, we don't have to produce all the goods and services we want to consume.

Terrible Tariffs

Having seen how trade makes us wealthier, let's now peer through the opportunity cost lens to examine how tariffs make our society poorer, on the whole. We can start by asking the first question on the minds of many as they read this.

What about those Detroit car makers who lose their jobs in the story of the magical wheat-to-car machine? I've even heard it argued that tariffs help maintain robust, middle-class families, the sorts of folks working for the Detroit automakers. Is this a justifiable claim? I don't think so.

Take the case of steel tariffs that have been politically popular in recent times. Yes, steel tariffs can secure some domestic steelworkers' jobs—but tremendous downsides accompany this policy. After all, if steelworkers lose their jobs through international trade, they don't become permanently unemployed. They find other jobs. The machines and the land they're sitting on start getting used to produce other items we desire. Without the tariffs, we get both cheap, foreign steel and whatever these workers could make instead.

I don't want to minimize the suffering of someone who loses their income due to trade with people in other nations. But, at the same time, it's important to understand a few points about this event.

First, someone losing a job from international trade is no different, from an economic perspective, than someone losing a job due to the routine, competitive process that characterizes all free economies. The alternative to this competitive process is public policy that freezes all producers in their current lines of production and employment, leading to total economic stagnation. Losing your job isn't fun. However, in the long run, the risk is better than living in a static system that doesn't allow for innovation.

As we saw in the last chapter, keeping relevant alternatives front and center is key. Would you prefer to live in a society that is permanently frozen at a horse-and-buggy level of technology, or even earlier transportation technology? I know there are some Luddites who'd take the bet, but it's not most of us.

Secondly, the empirical evidence, across many centuries, suggests that even displaced workers experience a higher living standard from trade over the long run.

I'll give you one example. With the invention of looms during the Industrial Revolution, many textile workers lost their jobs. But, amazingly, it wasn't long before their real standards of living rose due to the falling price of clothing that the mechanized loom precipitated.

So who's to say what the actual cost of protecting the domestic steel industry is? All we can say with confidence is that American steelworkers and machines would produce something else in the absence of tariff protection. We won't get that "something else" if workers and machines are "trapped" into making steel by the protective tariffs.

It doesn't take any economic eyeglasses to see that we could save jobs in the domestic steel industry by preventing Americans from buying cheaper, better foreign steel. Of course, we also could've saved jobs in the horse-and-buggy industry by tossing Henry Ford in jail for innovating the way he did.

What would the opportunity cost of this protection be? Protecting the buggy industry means we'd never have gotten the car. But that's not the only channel through which tariffs impoverish us. When a tariff raises the cost of steel, that crimps every domestic, steel-using producer.

They're unable to produce as much without access to the cheaper, foreign steel. Many of them adjust by laying off workers, including middle-class folks, who tariffs are supposedly implemented to help.

In the case of the recent round of steel tariffs in the U.S., this isn't simply speculation. A recent paper by economists Aaron Flaaen and Justin Pierce examines the March 2018 steel and aluminum tariffs.[61] On net, the tariffs cost jobs.

Yes, there was a "job-saving" effect (not necessarily a good thing—see above), but this was swamped by the tariff's "job-destroying" effects. The "job-saving" effect can be seen. The "job-destroying" effects must be foreseen.

The tariffs destroyed jobs for two reasons. First, the tariffs incited retaliatory tariffs that slammed domestic exports. Second, the increase in input costs (steel is used in thousands of production processes) sufficiently harmed other domestic industries, and many responded by contracting employment. This latter effect was even more significant than the backlash of retaliatory tariffs. In other words, our tariffs were the main culprit.

Wearing our economic eyeglasses, we realize that the argument for tariffs is just the broken window fallacy in a new garb. What might those laid-off workers have done with their salaries if they hadn't lost their jobs? As we saw in Chapter One, jobs aren't valuable for their own sake; they are valuable only when they produce things that help people achieve their goals. But maybe, just maybe, these laid-off employees would have started their own business out of their savings. Maybe they'd have invested in someone else's enterprise.

This is why I say tariffs don't contribute to preserving healthy middle-class families, at least not on net. A tariff might benefit some middle-class families but at the expense of other middle-class families. It's easy to see the families who benefit from the tariffs. It takes your economic eyeglasses to detect all the other families who lose due to tariffs.

True, the disemployed will find other jobs, just like those displaced by free trade. The difference is that this time, there's no net win.

Concentrated Benefits; Dispersed Costs

This brief discussion of steel tariffs allows us to answer a question that should be on your mind: If tariffs make us worse off, and if economists repeatedly warn about them, why do virtually all governments impose them?[62]

Take the case of American sugar tariffs. Suppose, for the sake of argument, that there are only ten U.S. sugar producers. They're shielded from foreign competition by tariffs. Now imagine that a senator from a state that doesn't produce any sugar, say, Maine, proposes a repeal of the tariffs. After all, he argues, without the tariffs, Americans will enjoy cheaper, higher-quality foreign sugar.

If the government repeals the tariff, every sugar consumer in the U.S.—everyone, by the way—will be a bit wealthier because we'd purchase the cheaper, foreign sugar. Meanwhile, the ten sugar producers stand to lose millions from repealing the tariff. Who do you think will show up to argue their case before Congress? The consumers, who each stand to gain ten bucks annually from tariff repeal? Or the sugar producers who stand to lose millions every year?

To ask that question is to answer it. The sugar producers will hire lobbyists; they'll develop economically erroneous, pro-tariff arguments for the relevant congressional sub-committee; they may even offer bribes in countries where corruption is prevalent. They will resort to economic lies.

This disastrous situation is what economists call the logic of "concentrated benefits and dispersed costs." Tariffs concentrate considerable benefits on the ten sugar producers. And sure, they pay a bit more for sugar in their role as consumers, but the income from tariffs dwarfs marginally higher prices at the grocery store.

Meanwhile, the cost of the tariffs—in the form of slightly higher sugar prices—is dispersed across 320 million sugar-consuming Americans. Any other American producer who uses sugar—and quite a few do—also shoulders part of the cost. To any individual consumer, the cost is relatively small. Would you march to Washington to campaign for sugar to be a few cents cheaper? I wouldn't.

This logic explains how we tend to get competition-restricting tariffs—even though our society would be wealthier without them.

Goods or Soldiers?

In this chapter, we've learned an important truth: Trade isn't war. Yet, there is a causal connection between trade and actual warfare. Once again, you can see it by looking through the opportunity cost lens. Economists have long argued that trade between nations is a powerful deterrent to war.

A somewhat obscure nineteenth-century economist Otto T. Mallery gave us one of my favorite aphorisms: "If goods don't cross borders, armies will." This pithy phrase captures an important insight.

Only someone looking through the opportunity cost lens would express this sentiment. The key is to see that trade between countries raises the opportunity cost of violent conflict. If the two countries' citizens are engaged in trade, war will cause their living standards to fall. The specter of falling living standards, in turn, may compel citizens to put pressure on their political leaders to avoid conflict.

This opportunity cost insight has empirical support. In a 2007 paper, Jun Xiang and his coauthors examine the relationship between international trade and warfare.[63] Their paper controls for a host of variables, such as whether the trading countries possess democratic governance. They find that trade between nations has what they call a significant "pacifying effect" on the countries' tendency to initiate conflict. The finding makes sense, given that war will eliminate many, if not all, gains from trade that the citizens of these countries enjoy.

In this chapter, we've seen that trade is not war. War results in mutual impoverishment. Trade results in mutual enrichment. Additionally, we've seen that impeding trade through tariffs makes us poorer and lowers the opportunity cost of initiating actual warfare. If you remember back to my first chapter, you'll recall that warfare also impoverishes us. So score another point for trade.

Throughout the last two chapters, we've seen how exchange makes people better off. But we haven't yet addressed many other questions that people have about markets. For example, many people wonder if markets open the door to fraud and discrimination. In short, doesn't just about anything go in unregulated markets? The next and final chapter will address that critical question.

CHAPTER SIX

MARKETS ARE UNREGULATED

*Profit and loss are the instruments by means
of which the consumers keep a tight rein on all
entrepreneurial activities.*

~ Ludwig von Mises

Profit: Four-Letter Word?

In the last two chapters, we've been exploring the benefits of exchange. Some critics of exchange, though, aren't satisfied. They're suspicious of the seemingly unregulated exchange that's been our subject so far. What about fraud? What's to stop unscrupulous sellers from hoodwinking unsuspecting buyers?

What about discrimination? What prevents bigoted or racist employers from refusing to hire a member of a religious or racial group they dislike? In short, trade might make some people better off. But, on the other hand, might it also be true that unregulated markets open the door to all sorts of other social ills?

Lurking behind concerns like this is another economic lie. This lie holds that "free markets" are synonymous with "unregulated markets." In this chapter, I'll argue that there is no such thing as an "unregulated market." There has never been, and there never will be.

All markets are regulated, only perhaps not in the way you're thinking. Furthermore, this regulation plays a vital role in reducing the extent of fraud and discrimination.

As we'll see in this chapter, not only does the profit-and-loss system mitigate the impulse to defraud and discriminate, but it also serves as a guide for all production processes. Why, for instance, don't we produce more medicine, more books, more chocolate, or more of any of the other good things in life? Because we'd have to withdraw scarce machinery and labor from production processes that create more value to do so. For a refresher on scarcity, revisit Chapter Two.

The profit-and-loss system means that markets aren't the chaotic arenas that most people perceive. Then again, most people aren't wearing economic eyeglasses, either.

Here's how economist Israel Kirzner puts it in his book, *Market Theory and the Price System*: "To the casual observer, market activity seems to be a bewildering and uncoordinated mass of transactions. Each individual in the market society is free to buy what and when he pleases, to sell what and when he pleases, to produce or to consume what he pleases, or to refrain altogether from any or all of these activities."[64]

That's a mouthful, but he's being intentionally comprehensive. Pay close attention to what he says next: "Economic analysis reveals that this seeming chaos in the activity of market participants is only apparent. In fact, analysis shows that the exchanges that take place are subject to definite forces at work in the market. These market forces guide the individuals participating in the market in their decisions."

What are these "forces"? How do they "regulate" market exchange? How do they curtail fraud and discrimination?

The answers might surprise you. The "regulations" I have in mind are "profits" and "losses." It's true; most don't think of "profits" or "losses" as "regulators"—but that's because they're not looking through the opportunity cost lens. For many people, the word "profit" is a four-letter word.

Why, then, is it helpful to think of "profits" and "losses" as an under-appreciated method of regulating market activity? This mental reframing is instructive because it's the lure of profits and the threat of losses that ultimately discipline buyers' and sellers' behavior.

Let me offer a brief example. Suppose a world-famous entrepreneur, such as the late Steve Jobs, had imagined that what consumers want is an iPhone made of solid platinum—the "iPlat," if you will. Based on this hunch, Jobs buys several tons of platinum, manufactures 10 million phones with it, and attempts to sell his new creations for fifty thousand dollars per phone. He chooses that price because at any lower amount, he won't cover his production costs.

I'm no entrepreneur myself, but I think it's safe to say that our hypothetical, harebrained Steve Jobs would suffer losses in this scenario. Hardly anyone wants to pay fifty thousand dollars for an iPhone, even for an indestructible phone made of platinum. If Jobs had gone through with this plan, consumers likely would have "punished" his behavior. They'd force him to endure losses by not buying his phone in sufficient numbers.

In essence, by forcing Jobs to experience losses, consumers would be rhetorically asking Jobs a question of sorts. They'd be asking him why he deprived them of the use of platinum in dental appliances and jewelry, two contexts where consumers do value platinum's use.

When Jobs uses platinum for his phones, we can't use that same platinum in its other, more valuable uses, such as in dental appliances that make our lives more pleasant. And as consumers, we would demonstrate our displeasure with that outcome by forcing losses on Jobs. That sounds a bit impersonal or mysterious. All I mean is that we wouldn't buy the iPlat in sufficient numbers to give Jobs what he's after: profits.

The reason Jobs never tried to give us the iPlat is because he anticipated he'd earn losses. In other words, the threat of loss was regulating, guiding, and even changing the actions he was taking.

Even if it were Jobs' lifelong aspiration to build a phone out of platinum, he would have restrained that impulse. His restraint was due to the profit-and-loss system. This sounds like regulation to me.

Monkfish

How does the profit-and-loss system also temper the impulse toward fraud and discrimination? First, fraud. Suppose you want a haircut. Once you're in the barber's seat, you describe your vision for the finished product. The barber nods as if he understands. Next, he picks up a razor and shaves you completely bald. You feel as if the whole experience is over before you can blink. Then, without missing a beat, he says, "That'll be 25 bucks. Thanks for your business. See you next month!"

You'd be shocked at his gall after he so brazenly defrauded you.

We could imagine other, similarly disturbing scenes. For example, you go to your favorite exquisite seafood restaurant where you order an expensive lobster. An hour later, the waiter brings out a plate of "monkfish"—more commonly known as "poor man's lobster." As you may know, monkfish is a cheap lobster substitute that tastes and even looks like a lobster. Half an hour later, the waiter reappears with the fifty-dollar check. Fraud.

Both of these scenarios should seem a bit far-fetched—even though we've all occasionally had the lousy haircut or patronized the disappointing restaurant. But why are my stories so improbable? Think about it for a moment. After all, it seems that a barber's profits would rise if he simply gave everyone a buzz cut. Perhaps he could service twenty customers a day instead of just six or seven.

At first glance, it might also seem that the restaurant's profits would rise by serving the cheap monkfish while charging for the expensive lobster. So why isn't virtually every seafood restaurant promising lobster and then serving monkfish? What stops the barber or the restaurant from taking advantage of you? Is it because they know you have your lawyer on speed-dial?

Of course not. The costs of using the court system far outweigh any damages the courts might award you for a fraudulent meal or haircut. What's worse is that the restaurant owner and barber know this, just as well as you and I. Armed with this knowledge, what stops sellers from defrauding you every time you exchange with them?

Conscience constrains many sellers. They couldn't look at themselves in the mirror if they lived their lives as frauds. But, unfortunately, that still leaves those who don't have a tender conscience and are just out to make a quick buck. Doesn't their profit-seeking positively cause them to defraud you? In what sense is profit going to curtail their impulse to deception? Wouldn't it only pour gasoline on the fire?

To answer that question, look through the opportunity cost lens with me. One force that disciplines sellers' fraudulent impulse is the threat of earning losses in the future. After all, none of us buyers would patronize this barber or restaurant again if we received the buzzcut or the monkfish.

So if he defrauds us, the seller will lose all the future profits he could have made from cutting our hair or serving our meals. Besides that, we'll probably tell all our friends and post about our terrible experiences on such platforms as Yelp.

I like to think about it this way. The "shadow of the future" looms over every exchange like a specter threatening to take away future profits. But you need to be wearing your economic eyeglasses to see that far ahead. If the barber wants to keep earning profits into the future, he'll "behave" in the present. The evaporation of future profits is the opportunity cost of misbehaving today.

That fact won't be enough to discipline every barber, but it does raise the cost of fraud for every barber. Over time, fraudulent barbers simply won't last. Losses will weed them from the market system, just as a gardener plucks dandelions from his flowerbed.

Rings and Promises

There's a way to make this logic even more robust. A barber might tell you that he'll provide a high-quality haircut, but how do you know he places a high value on your future business? Just how serious is the threat of losing future profits to him? Some fly-by-night barbers might simply be out to make a quick buck. Those aren't the barbers you want to patronize.

Quality assurance is important because if buyers suspect that the barber won't follow through, they'll be suspicious and avoid him. Such is the case, even if he's a high-quality, honest barber. As a result of the buyer's suspicion, neither party benefits from the trading discussed in the last two chapters.

To overcome buyer suspicions, sellers can offer so-called credible commitments to prospective buyers. As we'll see in a moment, these enable buyers and sellers to enjoy the gains more fully.

A credible commitment is anything that makes a promisor's word more believable. It does this by raising the promisor's opportunity cost of acting contrary to the other party's best interest. I realize that's an abstract description—so what's an example?

My favorite example comes from Notre Dame economist and legal scholar Margaret Brinig. In her 1990 paper, "Rings and Promises," she compellingly argues that engagement rings served as credible commitments to marry in the United States during the mid-twentieth century.[65]

Brinig notes that before 1935, American women could sue a fiancée who'd broken his engagement promise. The courts would usually award monetary damages to the woman to compensate her for wedding preparation expenses and shame.

In 1935, Indiana struck down its "breach of promise" laws (also called "heartbalm remedies"). By 1945, sixteen other states had followed Indiana's lead, with every other state eventually eliminating these provisions from the books. However, at the time, there existed a significant social stigma for a woman who experienced a broken engagement. Consequently, women still wanted a way to separate frivolous from serious suitors. A worst-case scenario for a woman was finding herself high and dry after an unserious man promised to marry her and then got cold feet.

What was the solution? Brinig argues that engagement ring–giving arose shortly after 1935 as a way for a man to demonstrate the credibility of his marriage offer. After all, he'd just invested in a costly diamond ring that he'd forfeit if he broke his promise to marry. Giving an engagement ring was a credible commitment to marry because men who weren't serious didn't offer them.

Women now possessed a way of sifting the masculine wheat from the boyish chaff.

Here's another example. One of the most memorable scenes in classic literature colorfully illustrates why people invest in credible commitments. You've probably heard the story. It comes from *The Odyssey*.

Odysseus knows that anyone who hears the Sirens' beautiful song will jump overboard and be devoured by these alluring but man-eating creatures. Nevertheless, he wants to listen to their music, so he binds his hands to the mast of his ship, rendering himself incapable of jumping overboard.

A credible commitment does the same thing. It ties a person's hands by raising the opportunity cost of specific actions that would be enticing otherwise.

Look What You Made Me Do

What does any of this have to do with disciplining fraud in markets? Here's what: Sellers can "bind their hands to the mast"—in a manner of speaking—by offering credible commitments to behave honestly with buyers.

Advertising often serves this function. Have you ever wondered why firms spend so much money on celebrity endorsements? As one notable example, in 2014, Coca-Cola signed a 26 million dollar contract with Taylor Swift to promote their products.[66] Are consumers more likely to

CHAPTER SIX: MARKETS ARE UNREGULATED

grab a Coke just because Swift films herself drinking one? And don't we all know she's drinking one only because Coca-Cola has paid her big bucks to do so?

The economic explanation for this curious phenomenon goes like this. Sellers aren't tricking weak-willed buyers by splashing celebrity images over their products. Instead, a celebrity endorsement is a costly investment that sellers recoup only if they uphold their commitment to quality. When consumers see the catchy Taylor Swift ad, they know that the Coca-Cola Company has spent tens of millions on this endorsement.

Furthermore, what will happen to Coca-Cola if the company begins diluting its flagship product to cut costs? Customers will stop buying as much Coke. And if that happens, Coca-Cola will never recoup the tremendous investment they made in the Swift contract. They'll be out tens of millions of dollars.

In other words, these massive investments serve as credible commitments to maintain quality into the future. Coca-Cola just raised the opportunity cost of diluting its product. As Taylor Swift herself might say, "Look what you made me do." Ultimately, consumers' demands and concerns force this curious behavior on companies like Coca-Cola. They want it as an assurance.

For the advertising mechanism to undergird quality, must consumers be walking around with a sophisticated understanding of economic forces rattling around inside their brains? No—or else they wouldn't need this book.

Benjamin Klein and Keith Leffler address this question in a famous 1981 paper:

We obviously do not want to claim that consumers 'know' this theory in the sense that they can verbalize it but only that they behave in such a way as if they recognize the forces at work. They may, for example, know from past experience that when a particular type of investment is present such as advertising they are much less likely to be deceived.[67]

Advertising is but one of many ways that sellers can offer credible commitments to buyers. I'll mention just one more. Premium restaurant owners often locate in high-rent areas of their city. This locational decision functions as a signal to consumers. Restaurants will recoup those high rents only if they don't renege on their quality commitment.

If they do renege, buyers will "punish" the owners by refusing to patronize the restaurant. If you're a restaurant owner who's paying a pretty penny for rent, losing patrons isn't something you can afford. Consequently, you do what you can to keep your promise of serving high-quality cuisine. No monkfish here.

To sum up, the lure of profits often prompts sellers to invest in credible commitments. The threat of losses disciplines their temptation to defraud us. None of this means that fraud never happens. Of course, it does. But the profit-and-loss system raises the cost of fraud and reduces its frequency. It's in this sense that "profits" and "losses" regulate market participants' behavior. Yes, there's a sense in which sellers can "do whatever they want." They won't be around for long if they do.

Economic Profits and Prophets

When you've mastered the economic way of thinking, wearing your economic eyeglasses will feel second nature. You'll often forget you're wearing them.

I'm not all the way there myself. Like most of us, I'm a work-in-progress. But many of those I look up to most had all but grafted the eyeglasses onto their face.

When you get there, you see things that others don't. You see before and farther than others do. I'm tempted to say it turns you into a bit of a prophet, able to foresee the consequences of events and policies, to which others remain oblivious.

In this second-to-last section of the book, I want to give you a sense of what I mean. To do it, we'll see how the profit-and-loss system raises employers' costs of practicing racial or sexual discrimination.

Remember Chapter Three. When something becomes more costly, people do less of it. Yes, that logic applies even to the basest, most deep-rooted impulses that afflict the human species. So simple, yet so far from simplistic.

Imagine a job that pays forty thousand dollars a year. Further, imagine that the employer dislikes people with blue eyes. He simply can't stand them. To make the example easy, suppose that there are just two applicants for this job. One has green eyes and will contribute forty-five thousand dollars annually to the employer's bottom line. The other has the dreaded blue eyes—but he'll contribute fifty thousand dollars to the employer's bottom line. The blue-eyed worker is simply more skilled.

Can the employer indulge his prejudice by hiring the green-eyed worker simply because his eyes are green? Of course, he can. We're talking about a voluntary exchange.

This decision will cost the employer. It will cost him five thousand dollars every year that he indulges his bigotry. So the question then becomes: Is the employer willing to pay five thousand dollars annually just to satisfy his vile tastes? Is he willing to incur that opportunity cost?

Suppose he does decide to gratify his bigoted impulse at the expense of the more productive worker. That only means there's a profit opportunity for a fair-minded rival to hire the more productive worker and begin outcompeting the prejudiced employer. In other words, the rivalry between employers exerts competitive pressure to eliminate discriminatory hiring practices.

I want you to notice something else that is implicit in this logic. We should expect less discrimination the more costly it becomes. This logic means that we'll tend to encounter less discrimination at higher salary rates. Thus, hiring custodial staff based on prejudice will only cost pennies out of the employer's profit.

By contrast, imagine hiring a CEO based on eye color, skin color, sex, religious creed, or other characteristics irrelevant to skillfully directing a company. In this case, the results could be catastrophic. Hiring the wrong person could mean millions of dollars in foregone profits or even the company's eventual bankruptcy. In short, the more it cuts into a company's profits, the less discrimination we should expect.

There's good empirical evidence for the ideas we've just been discussing. In 1962, Armen Alchian, who wore some of the clearest and furthest-seeing economic eyeglasses in history, partnered with coauthor Reuben Kessel to publish a paper that empirically explored how profits discipline discrimination.[68]

So steeped in the economic of way of thinking, Alchian had a hunch about the distribution of discrimination that ninety-nine percent of the human race would have overlooked.

NO FREE LUNCH   ■   CALEB S. FULLER

Alchian and Kessel begin their analysis by noting that law prohibits firms from keeping all their profits in some industries. The significance of this fact is that when firms can't keep all their profits, the opportunity cost of discrimination necessarily falls.

Think back to the example from a few moments ago. We said that the employer could make five thousand dollars in additional profit if he hired the disliked blue-eyed worker. Now suppose that the government confiscates every last penny of that five thousand dollars. Under that sort of regime, there'd no longer be an advantage in selecting the blue-eyed worker over the favored green-eyed worker. So the question is: In what industries do regulations block firms from keeping all their profits?

Examples include public utilities such as water, gas, and electricity companies. In these areas, enterprises are subject to profit regulations so that the rate of return can never rise above some government-stipulated minimum. Similar considerations have applied, at times, to railroads, buses, airlines, and taxis.

Alchian and Kessel remark about firms in these industries, "If [these firms] are able to earn more than the permissible pecuniary rate of return, then 'inefficiency' is a free good, because the alternative to inefficiency is the same pecuniary income and no 'inefficiency.'"

Unfortunately, so-called "inefficiency" may include indulging one's racial preferences.

That's what Alchian and Kessel find empirically. They examine employment data in different American industries. Specifically, they look at the proportion of Jewish employees across sectors during the first part of the twentieth century—a time when many strongly discriminated against Jews in the United States.

To examine Jewish employment, they compare the share of Jewish to non-Jewish Harvard Business School grads employed across various fields. What they learn is consistent with the logic of profit and loss. First, they find that the relative share of Jewish to non-Jewish grads is thirty-six percent overall in the ten industries they examine. However—and crucially—in the industries subject to the strictest profit regulation, they discover that the share of Jewish to non-Jewish employment drops to eighteen percent.

That sort of difference is what we'd expect because limiting a firm's ability to earn profits lowers the opportunity cost of discrimination. If you can't keep your extra profits, hiring the best worker doesn't make sense. You might as well hire a worker based on racial preference.

To those who have wholeheartedly embraced the opportunity cost lens, those findings might be disappointing, but they're not surprising. Economics shows us that the freer the profit-and-loss system is, the less fraud and discrimination we'll have. Markets certainly don't eliminate every last instance of discrimination, but contrast their performance with public efforts. Chapter

Three explored a public policy that seeks to reduce bias but only exacerbated discriminatory hiring practices.

In sum, profits and losses regulate the behavior of market participants. To perceive this regulatory function of profit and loss, we need to be wearing our economic eyeglasses. The argument has never been that the profit-and-loss system eliminates fraud or discrimination. Remember back to our barber and monkfish examples. The real question is: Why not more fraud and discrimination in a world filled with frauds and discriminators?

Economic Eyeglasses

The receptionist will see you in the lobby now. Your exam is finished. We're processing your script; your new glasses will be here in just a moment.

It wasn't that bad, right?

Disabusing oneself of economic lies can be an uncomfortable process. It was for me when I first began. That's because thinking clearly, thinking economically, can mount serious challenges to commonly held and widely cherished beliefs about how the social world operates.

But I've found that the payoff of clearer economic eyesight is oh-so worth it. That's why I keep going back for my annual check-up, back to the basics, to ensure my myopia hasn't overpowered my view of things.

If I've done my job, then I've demonstrated just how far you can get with a single, straightforward economic principle: opportunity cost. If all you know about economics is the concept of "opportunity cost," you know enough to see through many economic lies.

Their (imperfect) grasp of this simple yet profound concept is one reason why economists tend to agree on a broad number of issues. It's the reason we can call out economists for when they fail to live up to the principles they once professed.

Wearing the opportunity cost lens, you won't fall for the canards that war—any war—boosts the economy or that rent control is a free lunch for tenants. Instead, you'll be wary of well-intentioned public policies as you scrutinize how they change the costs and the benefits people face. You can now identify the mutual benefit in exchange and some of the self-regulating properties of the profit-and-loss system.

More than anything, I hope this short book has given you your first pair of economic eyeglasses. Unlike most glasses, I've never really found a reason to take them off. Wear them when you're reading, wear them when you're sleeping, wear them in the shower. Keep them polished. You never know the next time life may throw a shortsighted economic claim—an economic lie—your way.

NOTES

1. Usually attributed to Herbert Spencer.

2. Optometrists excepted.

3. https://www.nytimes.com/2001/09/14/opinion/reckonings-after-the-horror.html

4. Henry Hazlitt, *Economics in One Lesson: The Shortest and Surest Way to Understand Basic Economics* (Knoxville, TN: Crown Publishing Group, 2010 [original publication: 1946]).

5. https://www.econlib.org/library/Bastiat/basEss.html?chapter_num=4#book-reader

6. Paul H. Rubin, "Folk Economics," *Southern Economic Journal* (July 1, 2003), 157–171.

7. James M. Buchanan, "Economics and Its Scientific Neighbors," *The Structure of Economic Science: Essays on Methodology.* (Englewood Cliffs, NJ: Prentice-Hall, 1966), 166–183.

8. Deirdre N. McCloskey, *The Applied Theory of Price* (New York: Macmillan Publishing Company, 1985).

9. https://www.econlib.org/library/Bastiat/basEss.html?chapter_num=4#book-reader

10. Henry David Thoreau, *Walden and Other Writings* (New York: Bantam Classics, 1981).

11. https://www.politico.com/story/2011/08/irene-an-economic-blow-or-boost-062206

12. Solomon M. Hsiang and Amir S. Jina, "The Causal Effect of Environmental Catastrophe on Long-Run Economic Growth: Evidence from 6,700 Cyclones," *National Bureau of Economic Research*, No. w20352 (2014).

13. Robert Higgs, "Wartime Prosperity? A Reassessment of the US Economy in the 1940s," *The Journal of Economic History*, 52, no. 1 (1992), 41–60.

14. For a visual of what happens to "overall GDP" compared to "private GDP" in the United States during World War II, see this essay by economist Robert Murphy: https://www.theamericanconservative.com/articles/the-myth-of-wartime-prosperity/. In the article, Murphy leans on original work by Robert Higgs including the following book: Robert Higgs, *Depression, War, and Cold War: Challenging the Myths of Conflict and Prosperity* (Oxford University Press, 2006). Also, see this paper: Steven Horwitz and Michael J. McPhillips, "The Reality of the Wartime Economy: More Historical Evidence on Whether World War II Ended the Great Depression," *The Independent Review*, 17, no. 3 (2013), 325–347.

15. https://www.econlib.org/archives/2013/09/israel_kirzner_conversation.html

16. Originally recounted in Vilfredo Pareto, *The Mind and Society* (New York: Harcourt, Brace and Company, 1916).

17. Richard Langworth, *Churchill by Himself: The Definitive Collection of Quotations* (New York: Public Affairs, 2011).

18. https://www.creators.com/read/thomas-sowell/02/07/priceless-politics-part-ii

19. Jimmy McMillan thinks so: https://en.wikipedia.org/wiki/Jimmy_McMillan

20. Steven NS Cheung, "Roofs or Stars: The Stated Intents and Actual Effects of a Rents Ordinance," *Economic Inquiry*, 13, no. 1 (1975), 1–21.

21. https://www.igmchicago.org/surveys/rent-control/

22. Robert L. Schuettinger and Eamonn F. Butler, *Forty Centuries of Wage and Price Controls: How Not to Fight Inflation* (Auburn, AL: Ludwig von Mises Institute, 1979).

23. https://fee.org/resources/roofs-or-ceilings-the-current-housing-problem/

24. https://history.fee.org/publications/no-vacancies/

25. See Rydenfelt's paper in: https://www.fraserinstitute.org/sites/default/files/RentControlMythsRealities.pdf

26. See the following book for a discussion of arson and rent control in New York City: William Tucker, *Zoning, Rent Control, and Affordable Housing* (Washington, DC: Cato Institute, 1991), 43.

27. See Lindbeck quoted here: https://www.npr.org/sections/money/2019/03/05/700432258/the-return-of-rent-control

28. https://www.fraserinstitute.org/sites/default/files/RentControlMythsRealities.pdf

29. Steven NS Cheung, "Roofs or Stars: The Stated Intents and Actual Effects of a Rents Ordinance," *Economic Inquiry*, 13, no. 1 (1975), 1–21.

30. For more crazy examples, see David S. Lucas and Caleb S. Fuller, "Bounties, Grants, and Market-Making Entrepreneurship," *The Independent Review*, 22, no. 4 (2018), 507–528. See also David S. Lucas, Caleb S. Fuller, and Ennio E. Piano, "Rooking the State," *International Review of Law and Economics*, 55 (2018), 12–20.

31. Michael G. Vann, "Of Rats, Rice, and Race: The Great Hanoi Rat Massacre, an Episode in French Colonial History," *French Colonial History*, 4, no. 1 (2003), 191–203.

32. Roger LeRoy Miller, Daniel K. Benjamin, and Douglass Cecil North, The Economics of Public Issues (Boston, MA: Addison-Wesley, 2003).

33. Unless, like my freshman year college roommate, you refer to chicken as "the bastard child of the meat department." His demand for steak was relatively inelastic.

34. https://www.washingtonpost.com/archive/business/1993/07/16/how-to-sink-an-industry-and-not-soak-the-r ich/08ea5310-4a4b-4674-ab88-fad8c42cf55b/

35. German economist Horst Siebert coined this term.

36. Richard B. McKenzie and Gordon Tullock, *The New World of Economics: A Remake of a Classic for New Generations of Economics Students* (New York: Springer Science+Business Media, 2012).

37. See pages 58–63 in McKenzie and Tullock for a comprehensive look at the episode I describe here.

38. Ibid.

39. Garrick Blalock, Vrinda Kadiyali, and Daniel H. Simon, "Driving Fatalities after 9/11: A Hidden Cost of Terrorism," *Applied Economics*, 41, no. 14 (2009), 1717–1729.

40. Jennifer L. Doleac and Benjamin Hansen, "The Unintended Consequences of 'Ban the Box': Statistical Discrimination and Employment Outcomes when Criminal Histories are Hidden," *Journal of Labor Economics*, 38, no. 2 (2020), 321–374.

41. https://www.brookings.edu/research/occupational-licensing-and-the-american-worker/

42. For anyone interested, the application can be found here: https://www.annapolis.gov/DocumentCenter/View/860/Fortune-Telling-License-Application-pdf

43. Sidney L. Carroll and Robert J. Gaston, "Occupational Restrictions and the Quality of Service Received: Some Evidence," *Southern Economic Journal* (1981), 959–976.

44. Shirley Svorny, "Licensing Doctors: Do Economists Agree?" *Econ Journal Watch*, 1, no. 2 (2004), 279–305; and Daniel B. Klein, William L. Davis, and David Hedengren, "Economics

Professors' Voting, Policy Views, Favorite Economists, and Frequent Lack of Consensus," *Econ Journal Watch*, 10, no. 1 (2013), 116–125.

45. James M. Buchanan, "Game Theory, Mathematics, and Economics," *Journal of Economic Methodology*, 8, no. 1 (2001), 27–32.

46. Ludwig von Mises, *Human Action* (Auburn, AL: Ludwig von Mises Institute, 1998 [1949]). See page 195.

47. https://plato.stanford.edu/entries/exploitation/

48. https://www.gutenberg.org/files/3600/3600-h/3600-h.htm

49. Ludwig von Mises, *Human Action* (Auburn, AL: Ludwig von Mises Institute, 1998 [1949]), 660.

50. Benjamin Powell, *Out of Poverty: Sweatshops in the Global Economy* (Cambridge, UK: Cambridge University Press, 2014).

51. Jeff R. Clark and Benjamin Powell, "Sweatshop Working Conditions and Employee Welfare: Say It Ain't Sew," *Comparative Economic Studies*, 55, no. 2 (2013), 343–357.

52. See economist Max Roser's colorful displays to orient yourself about the past and present of global poverty: https://ourworldindata.org/extreme-poverty

53. https://www.econlib.org/library/Bastiat/basEss.html?chapter_num=4#book-reader

54. See the following textbook for a similar example: Paul T. Heyne, Peter J. Boettke, and David L. Prychitko, *The Economic Way of Thinking* (London: Pearson Education International, 2010).

55. Mallery is the most likely source of this quote. See here for more information on this disputed quotation: https://oll.libertyfund.org/page/did-bastiat-say-when-goods-don-t-cross-borders-soldiers-will

56. https://www.igmchicago.org/surveys/steel-and-aluminum-tariffs/

57. Kenneth E. Boulding, *Economic Analysis* (London: Harper and Brothers Publishers, 1941), 30. The example also appears

in Murray N. Rothbard, *Man, Economy, and State* (Auburn, AL: Ludwig von Mises Institute, 2009 [1962]) 98.

58. https://www.smithsonianmag.com/history/for-40-years-this-russian-family-was-cut-off-from-all-human-cont   act-unaware-of-world-war-ii-7354256/

59. Adam Smith, *The Wealth of Nations: An Inquiry into the Nature and Causes of the Wealth of Nations* (Petersfield, UK: Harriman House Limited, 2010 [1776]).

60. See a version of this story in Landsburg's famous book: Steven E. Landsburg, *The Armchair Economist: Economics & Everyday Life* (New York: Simon and Schuster, 2007).

61. Aaron Flaaen and Justin R. Pierce, "Disentangling the Effects of the 2018–2019 Tariffs on a Globally Connected US Manufacturing Sector" (2019). Working paper.

62. Besides the fact that the "Trade Is War" lie is popular with the American people. See economist Bryan Caplan's book for a sense of just how popular: Bryan Caplan, *The Myth of the Rational Voter* (Princeton, NJ: Princeton University Press, 2011).

63. Jun Xiang, Xiaohong Xu, and George Keteku, "Power: The Missing Link in the Trade Conflict Relationship," *Journal of Conflict Resolution*, 51, no. 4 (2007), 646–663.

64. Israel Mayer Kirzner, *Market Theory and the Price System* (Auburn, AL: Ludwig von Mises Institute, 2007 [1963]), 3.

65. Margaret F. Brinig, "Rings and Promises," *Journal of Law, Economics & Organization*, 6 (1990), 203.

66. https://www.hollywoodreporter.com/news/general-news/taylor-swift-scores-long-term-416139/

67. Benjamin Klein and Keith B. Leffler, "The Role of Market Forces in Assuring Contractual Performance," *Journal of Political Economy*, 89, no. 4 (1981), 615–641.

68. Armen A. Alchian and Reuben A. Kessel, "Competition, Monopoly and the Pursuit of Money," *Aspects of Labor Economics*, 14 (1962), 157–183.

CPSIA information can be obtained
at www.ICGtesting.com
Printed in the USA
LVHW021257310822
727185LV00003B/243